# R Data Science Essentials

Learn the essence of data science and visualization using R in no time at all

**Raja B. Koushik**

**Sharan Kumar Ravindran**

BIRMINGHAM - MUMBAI

# R Data Science Essentials

First published: January 2016

Production reference:1040116

Published by Packt Publishing Ltd.
Livery Place
35 Livery Street
Birmingham B32PB, UK.

ISBN 978-1-78528-654-4

www.packtpub.com

# Credits

**Authors**
Raja B. Koushik

Sharan Kumar Ravindran

**Reviewers**
Jeremy Gray

Navin K Manaswi

**Commissioning Editor**
Dipika Gaonkar

**Acquisition Editor**
Manish Nainan

**Content Development Editor**
Mehvash Fatima

**Technical Editor**
Suwarna Patil

**Copy Editor**
Tasneem Fatehi

**Project Coordinator**
Shipra Chawhan

**Proofreader**
Safis Editing

**Indexer**
Mariammal Chettiyar

**Graphics**
Disha Haria

**Production Coordinator**
Arvindkumar Gupta

**Cover Work**
Arvindkumar Gupta

# About the Authors

**Raja B. Koushik** is a business intelligence professional with over 7 years of experience and is currently working in one of the leading international IT services companies. His primary interest lies for business intelligence technologies, such as ETL, reporting, and dashboarding, along with analytics based on statistics. He has worked with one of the world's largest companies for both their U.S. as well as UK business in the healthcare and leasing domains. He holds an engineering degree with specialization in information technology from Anna University.

I would like to thank my friends, for I don't know how far I would have come without you guys. I would like to thank Sharan, for giving me this opportunity and also to the Packt team for their constant support. I would like to dedicate this book to Saranya, my wife, for always believing in me and for being so encouraging and supportive of my endeavours; to Shravani, my little bundle of joy, for all the joy and happiness that she has given me; last but not the least, to my parents, Mr Boopalan and Mrs Geetha, without you both I am nothing.

**Sharan Kumar Ravindran** is a data scientist with over 5 years of experience and is currently working with a leading e-commerce company in India. His primary interest lies in statistics and machine learning, and he has worked with multiple customers across Europe and the U.S. in the e-commerce and IoT domains. He holds an MBA degree with specialization in marketing and business analysis. He conducts workshops, partnering with Anna University, to train their staff, research scholars, and volunteers in analytics. In addition to co-authoring *Data Science Essentials with R* by *Packt Publishing*, Sharan has also co-authored *Mastering Social Media Mining with R* by *Packt Publishing*. He maintains www.rsharankumar.com, a website with links to his social profiles and data blog.

I would like to thank all my friends, colleagues, and family members, without whom I wouldn't have learned as much as I did. I would also like to thank the readers of my first book, *Mastering Social Media Mining*, whose feedback helped me a lot. I would like to specially thank my mother, dad, wife, and sister for all the support they provided. I would like to dedicate this book to my grandparents, son, and niece.

# About the Reviewers

**Jeremy Gray** is a data scientist with over 8 years of experience and is based in Toronto.

He completed his PhD in biology at the University of Auckland (the birthplace of R) and worked as a post-doctoral fellow and course instructor at the University of Toronto. His research interests are primarily in using R as an integrated machine learning environment, financial modeling, and consumer analytics, as well as pedagogical methods in scientific computing.

I would like to thank my wonderful fiancé, Mandy Cheema, for her support during the reviewing of this book.

**Navin K Manaswi** is a data science professional who loves to delve into messy complex data to bring meaningful insights out of it. Although he has been recognized as one of the top 10 data scientists in India, he still loves to learn everyday as a curious child does. Having done both his bachelor's and master's from IIT Kanpur, he has been contributing to the world of data analytics, machine learning, big data technologies, and business intelligence. So far, he has worked at the intersection of technologies and business domains of supply chain management, sales and marketing, finance, and healthcare.

I would like to thank my mother, Smt. Geeta, for invaluable guidance.

# www.PacktPub.com

## Support files, eBooks, discount offers, and more

For support files and downloads related to your book, please visit www.PacktPub.com.

Did you know that Packt offers eBook versions of every book published, with PDF and ePub files available? You can upgrade to the eBook version at www.PacktPub.com and as a print book customer, you are entitled to a discount on the eBook copy. Get in touch with us at service@packtpub.com for more details.

At www.PacktPub.com, you can also read a collection of free technical articles, sign up for a range of free newsletters and receive exclusive discounts and offers on Packt books and eBooks.

https://www2.packtpub.com/books/subscription/packtlib

Do you need instant solutions to your IT questions? PacktLib is Packt's online digital book library. Here, you can search, access, and readPackt's entire library of books.

## Why subscribe?

- Fully searchable across every book published by Packt
- Copy and paste, print, and bookmark content
- On demand and accessible via a web browser

## Free access for Packt account holders

If you have an account with Packt atwww.PacktPub.com, you can use this to access PacktLib today and view 9 entirely free books. Simply use your login credentials for immediate access.

# Table of Contents

# Preface

According to an article in *Harvard Business Review*, a data scientist's job is the best job of the 21st century. With the massive explosion in the amount of data generated, and with organizations becoming increasingly data-driven, the requirement for data science professionals is ever increasing.

*R Data Science Essentials* will provide a detailed step-by-step guide to cover various important concepts in data science. It covers concepts such as loading data from different sources, carrying out fundamental data manipulation techniques, extracting the hidden patterns in data through exploratory data analysis, and building complex, predictive, and forecasting models. Finally, you will learn to visualize and communicate the data analysis to an audience. This book is aimed at beginners and intermediate users of R, taking them through the most important techniques in data science that will help them start their data scientist journey.

## What this book covers

*Chapter 1, Getting Started with R*, introduces basic concepts such as loading the data to R from different sources, implementing various preprocessing techniques to handle missing data and outliers, and managing data from different sources by merging and subsetting it. It also covers arithmetic and string operations in R. Overall, this chapter will help you convert the data to a usable format that can be consumed for further data analysis and model building.

*Chapter 2, Exploratory Data Analysis*, introduces different statistical techniques that assist not only in the better understanding of the data, but also help in developing intuition about the dataset by summarizing and visualizing the important characteristics of the variables in the dataset.

*Chapter 3, Pattern Discovery*, focuses on techniques to extract patterns from the raw data as well as to derive sequential patterns hidden in the data. This chapter will touch on the evaluation metrics and the tweaking of parameters to adjust the rank of the association rules. This chapter also discusses the business cases where these techniques can be used.

*Chapter 4, Segmentation Using Clustering*, demonstrates how and when to perform a clustering analysis, how to identify the ideal number of clusters for a dataset, and how the clustering can be implemented using R. It also focuses on hierarchical clustering and how it is different from normal clustering. You will also learn about the visualization of clusters.

*Chapter 5, Developing Regression Models*, demonstrates why regression models are used and how logistic regression is different from linear regression. It shows you how to implement regression models using R and also explores the various methods used to check the fit accuracy. It touches on the different methodologies that can be used to improve the accuracy of the model.

*Chapter 6, Time Series Forecasting*, explains forecasting from fundamentals such as converting the normal data frame to a time series data and shows you methods that help uncover the hidden patterns in time series data. It will also teach you the implementation of different algorithms for the forecasting.

*Chapter 7, Recommendation Engine*, shows you the basic idea behind a recommendation engine and some of the real-life use cases in the first part of the chapter. In the latter part of the chapter, the popular collaborative filtering algorithm based on items as well as users is explained in detail along with its implementation.

*Chapter 8, Communicating Data Analysis*, covers some of the best ways to communicate the results to the user, such as how to make data visualization better using packages in R such as `ggplot` and `googleViz`, and demonstrates stitching together the visualizations by creating an interactive dashboard using R shiny.

# What you need for this book

In order to make your learning efficient, you need to have a computer with Windows, Ubuntu, or OS X.

You need to download R to execute the code mentioned in this book. You can download and install R using the CRAN website available at `http://cran.r-project.org/`. All the code was written using RStudio. RStudio is an **integrated development environment** (IDE) for R and can be downloaded from `http://www.rstudio.com/products/rstudio/`.

# Who this book is for

If you are an aspiring data scientist or analyst who has a basic understanding of data science and basic hands-on experience in R or any other analytics tool, then *R Data Science Essentials* is the book for you.

# Conventions

In this book, you will find a number of styles of text that distinguish between different kinds of information. Here are some examples of these styles, and an explanation of their meaning.

Any command-line input or output is written as follows:

```
data  <- read.delim("local-data.txt", header=TRUE, sep="\t")
data  <- read.table("local-data.txt", header=TRUE, sep="\t")
```

**New terms** and **important words** are shown in bold. Words that you see on the screen, for example, in menus or dialog boxes, appear in the text like this: "Clicking the Next button moves you to the next screen."

 Warnings or important notes appear in a box like this.

# Reader feedback

Feedback from our readers is always welcome. Let us know what you think about this book—what you liked or may have disliked. Reader feedback is important for us to develop titles that you really get the most out of.

To send us general feedback, simply send an e-mail to feedback@packtpub.com, and mention the book title via the subject of your message.

If there is a topic that you have expertise in and you are interested in either writing or contributing to a book, see our author guide on www.packtpub.com/authors.

# Customer support

Now that you are the proud owner of a Packt book, we have a number of things to help you to get the most from your purchase.

# Downloading the example code

You can download the example code files for all Packt books you have purchased from your account at http://www.packtpub.com. If you purchased this book elsewhere, you can visit http://www.packtpub.com/support and register to have the files e-mailed directly to you.

# Errata

Although we have taken every care to ensure the accuracy of our content, mistakes do happen. If you find a mistake in one of our books—maybe a mistake in the text or the code—we would be grateful if you would report this to us. By doing so, you can save other readers from frustration and help us improve subsequent versions of this book. If you find any errata, please report them by visiting http://www.packtpub.com/submit-errata, selecting your book, clicking on the **errata submission form** link, and entering the details of your errata. Once your errata are verified, your submission will be accepted and the errata will be uploaded on our website, or added to any list of existing errata, under the Errata section of that title. Any existing errata can be viewed by selecting your title from http://www.packtpub.com/support.

# Piracy

Piracy of copyright material on the Internet is an ongoing problem across all media. At Packt, we take the protection of our copyright and licenses very seriously. If you come across any illegal copies of our works, in any form, on the Internet, please provide us with the location address or website name immediately so that we can pursue a remedy.

Please contact us at copyright@packtpub.com with a link to the suspected pirated material.

We appreciate your help in protecting our authors, and our ability to bring you valuable content.

# Questions

You can contact us at questions@packtpub.com if you are having a problem with any aspect of the book, and we will do our best to address it.

# 1
# Getting Started with R

R is one of the most popular programming languages used in computation statistics, data visualization, and data science. With the increasing number of companies becoming data-driven, the user base of R is also increasing fast. R is supported by over two million users worldwide.

In this book, you will learn how to use R to load data from different sources, carry out fundamental data manipulation techniques, extract the hidden patterns in data through exploratory data analysis, and build complex predictive as well as forecasting models. Finally, you will learn to visualize and communicate the data analysis to the audience. This book is aimed at beginners and intermediate users of R, taking them through the most important techniques in data science that will help them start their data scientist journey.

In this chapter, we will be covering the basic concepts of R such as reading data from different sources, understanding the data format, learning about the preprocessing techniques, and performing basic arithmetic and string operations.

The objective of this chapter is to first help the reader get a hold on to programming in R and know about the basic operations that will be useful for any analysis. In this chapter, we will essentially be exploring the standard techniques that will be used to convert the raw data into a usable format.

The following topics will be covered in this chapter:

- Reading data from different sources
- Discussing data types in R
- Discussing data preprocessing techniques
- Performing arithmetic operations on the data

- Performing string operations on the data
- Discussing control structures in R
- Bringing the data into a usable format

# Reading data from different sources

Importing data to R is quite simple and can be done from multiple sources. The most common method of importing data to R is through the **comma-separated values (CSV)** format. The CSV data can be accessed through the read.csv function. This is the simplest way to read the data as it requires just a single line command and the data is ready. Depending on the quality of the data, it may or may not require processing.

```
data <- read.csv("c:/local-data.csv")
```

The other function similar to read.csv is read.csv2. This function is also used to read the CSV files but the difference is that read.csv2 is mostly used in the European countries, where comma is used as decimal point and semicolon is used as a separator. Also, the data can be read from R using a few more parameters, such as read.table and read.delim. By default, read.delim is used to read tab-delimited files, and the read.table function can be used to read any file by supplying suitable parameters as the input:

```
data  <- read.delim("local-data.txt", header=TRUE, sep="\t")
data  <- read.table("local-data.txt", header=TRUE, sep="\t")
```

> **Downloading the example code**
>
> You can download the example code files for all Packt books you have purchased from your account at http://www.packtpub.com. If you purchased this book elsewhere, you can visit http://www.packtpub.com/support and register to have the files e-mailed directly to you.

All the preceding functions can take multiple parameters that would explain the data source's format at best. Some of these parameters are as follows:

- header: This is a logical value indicating the presence of column names in the file. When it is set to TRUE, it indicates that the column names are present. By default, the value is considered as TRUE.
- sep: This defines the separator in the file. By default, the separator is comma for read.csv, tab for read.delim, and white space for the read.table function.

- nrows: This specifies the maximum number of rows to read from the file. By default, the entire file will be read.

- row.names: This will specify which column should be considered as a row name. When it is set as NULL, the row names will be forced as numbers. This parameter will take the column's position (one represents the first column) as input.

- fill: This parameter when set as TRUE can read the data with unequal row lengths and blank fields are implicitly added.

These are some of the common parameters used along with the functions to read the data from a file.

We have so far explored reading data from a delimited file. In addition to this, we can read data in Excel formats as well. This can be achieved using the xlsx or XLConnect packages. We will see how to use one of these packages in order to read a worksheet from a workbook:

```
install.packages("xlsx")
library(xlsx)
mydata <- read.xlsx("DTH AnalysisV1.xlsx", 1)
head(mydata)
```

In the preceding code, we first installed the xlsx package that is required to read the Excel files. We loaded the package using the library function, then used the read.xlsx function to read the excel file, and passed an additional parameter, 1, that specifies which sheet to read from the excel file.

# Reading data from a database

Apart from reading the data from a local file, R allows us to read the data from different sources and different formats. If we consider any enterprise setup, the data would mostly be present in a database. It will be complicated if we import the data from the database to a local file and then perform the analysis; we should be able to access the data directly from the source. This can be achieved using R.

First, let's see how to access data from a database. In order to read data from a database, we need to establish a connection with the database, which could reside in the local system or a remote server. We can establish the connection to the database using either ODBC or JDBC, which are R packages.

We will have a detailed look at accessing the data from the database using the JDBC method. In order to perform this operation, we need to install the RJDBC and sqldf packages. The RJDBC package is used to establish a connection with the database and the sqldf package is used to write the SQL queries:

```
install.packages("RJDBC")
library(RJDBC)
install.packages("sqldf")
library(sqldf)
```

We will now learn to establish a connection with the DB. We need to set up a few things in order to connect with the DB. To use the JDBC connection, we need to download the driver. The downloaded file will depend on the database to which we are going to connect, such as **SQL Server**, **Oracle**, or **PostgreSQL**.

In the following case, we will connect to a SQL server database. The JDBC driver can be downloaded from http://www.microsoft.com/en-in/download/details.aspx?id=11774 in order to provide connectivity. In the following code, we will pass the driver name as well as the location of the JAR file that comes with the download to the JDBC function. The JDBC function creates a new **DBI** driver that can be used to start the JDBC connection.

```
drv <- JDBC("com.microsoft.sqlserver.jdbc.SQLServerDriver", "C:/Users/
Downloads/Microsoft SQL Server JDBC Driver 3.0/sqljdbc_3.0/enu/sqljdbc4.
jar")
```

By using the dbConnect function, we establish the actual connection with the database. We need to pass the location of the database, username, and password to this function. On the successful execution of the following code, the connection will be established and we can check the connectivity using the dbGetQuery function:

```
conn <- dbConnect(drv, "jdbc:sqlserver://localhost;database=SAMPLE_DB",
"admin", "test")
bin <- dbGetQuery(conn, "select count(*) from  sampletable")
```

In addition to the relational databases, we can also connect and access the non-relational databases, such as **Cassandra, Hadoop, MongoDB,** and so on. We will now see how to access data from a Cassandra database. In order to access the data from a Cassandra database, we need to install the RCassandra package. The connection to the database can be made using the RC.connect function. We need to pass the host IP as well as the port number to establish the connection. Then finally, we need to specify the username and password as follows to establish the connection successfully:

```
library(RCassandra)
conn <- RC.connect(host = "localhost", port = 9160)
RC.login(conn, username = "user", password = "password123")
```

In Cassandra, the container for the application data is keyspace, which is similar to schema in the relational database. We can use the RC.describe.keyspaces function to get an understanding about the data, and then using the RC.use function, we select keyspace to be used for all the subsequent operations:

```
RC.describe.keyspaces(conn)
RC.use(conn, keyspace = "sampleDB", cache.def = TRUE)
```

We can read the data using the following code and once all the readings are done, we can close the connection using RC.close:

```
a<-RC.read.table(conn, c.family = "Users", convert = TRUE, na.strings =
"NA",
                 as.is = FALSE, dec = ".")
RC.close(conn)
```

We can discuss the RMongo package as well as it is quite popular.

Similarly, R has the ability to read data from a table in a website using the XML package. We can also read the data of **SAS**, **SPSS**, **Stata**, and **Systat** using the Hmisc package for SPSS and SAS and foreign for Stata and Systat.

For more details about the methodology of extracting the data from these sources, find the reference at the following URLs:

* http://www.statmethods.net/input/importingdata.html
* http://www.r-bloggers.com/importing-data-into-r-from-different-sources/

While establishing connectivity with a remote system, you could face a few issues related to security and others specific to the R version and package version. Most likely, the common issues would have been discussed in the forum, stackoverflow.

# Data types in R

We explored the various ways that we can read the data from R in the previous session. Let's have a look at the various data types that are supported by R. Before going into the details of the data type, we will first explore the variable data types in R.

# Variable data types

The common variable data types in R are numerical, integer, character, and logical. We will explore each one of them using R.

Numeric is the default variable type for all the variables holding numerical values in R:

```
a <- 10
class(a)
[1] "numeric"
```

In the preceding code, we actually passed an integer to the a variable but it is still being saved in a numeric format.

We can now convert this variable defined as a numeric in R into an integer using the as.integer function:

```
a <- as.integer(a)
class(a)
[1] "integer"
```

Similarly, here is a variable of the character and logical types:

```
name <- "Sharan"
class(name)
[1] "character"

# Logical Type
flag <- TRUE
class(flag)
[1] "logical"
```

Having explored the variable data types, now we will move up the hierarchy and explore these data types: vector, matrix, list, and dataframe.

A **vector** is a sequence of elements of a basic data type. It could be a sequence of numeric or logical characters. A vector can't have a sequence of elements with different data types. The following are the examples for the numeric, character, and logical vectors:

```
v1 <- c(12, 34, -21, 34.5, 100) # numeric vector
class(v1)
 [1] "numeric"
v2 <- c("sam", "paul", "steve",  "mark") # character vector
class(v2)
[1] "character"
v3 <- c(TRUE, FALSE, TRUE, FALSE, TRUE, FALSE) #logical vector
class(v3)
[1] "logical"
```

Now, let's consider the v1 numeric vector and the v2 character vector, combine these two, and see the resulting vector:

```
newV <- c(v1,v2)
class(newV)
[1] "character"
```

We can see that the resultant vector is a character vector; we will see what happened to the numeric elements of the first vector. From the following output, we can see that the numeric elements are now converted into character vectors represented in double quotes, whereas the numeric vector will be represented without any quotes:

```
newV
 [1] "12"      "34"      "-21"     "34.5"    "100"     "sam"     "paul"    "steve"
"mark"
```

A **matrix** is a collection of elements that has a two-dimensional representation, that is, columns and rows. A matrix can contain elements of the same data type only. We can create a matrix using the following code. First, we pass the intended row names and column names to the rnames and cnames variables, then using the matrix function, we will create the matrix. We specify the row names and column names using the dimnames parameter:

```
rnames <- c("R1", "R2", "R3", "R4", "R5")
cnames <- c("C1", "C2", "C3", "C4", "C5")
```

```
matdata <-matrix(1:25, nrow=5,ncol=5, dimnames=list(rnames, cnames))
class(matdata)
[1] "matrix"
typeof(matdata)
[1] "integer"
Matdata
C1 C2 C3 C4 C5
R1  1  6 11 16 21
R2  2  7 12 17 22
R3  3  8 13 18 23
R4  4  9 14 19 24
R5  5 10 15 20 25
```

A **list** is a sequence of data elements similar to a vector but can hold elements of different datatypes. We will combine the variables that we created in the vector section. As in the following code, these variables hold numeric, character, and logical vectors. Using the list function, we combine them, but their individual data type still holds:

l1 <- list(v1, v2, v3)

```
typeof(l1)
> l1
[[1]]
[1]  12.0  34.0 -21.0  34.5 100.0

[[2]]
[1] "sam"    "paul"  "steve" "mark"

[[3]]
[1]  TRUE FALSE  TRUE FALSE  TRUE FALSE
```

**Factors** are categorical variables in R, which means that they take values from a limited known set. In case of factor variables, R internally stores an equivalent integer value and maps it to the character string.

A **dataframe** is similar to the matrix, but in a data frame, the columns can hold data elements of different types. The data frame will be the most commonly used data type for most of the analysis. As any dataset would have multiple data points, each could be of a different type. R comes with a good number of built-in datasets such as `mtcars`. When we use sample datasets to cover the various examples in the coming chapters, you will get a better understanding about the data types discussed so far.

# Data preprocessing techniques

The first step after loading the data to R would be to check for possible issues such as missing data, outliers, and so on, and, depending on the analysis, the preprocessing operation will be decided. Usually, in any dataset, the missing values have to be dealt with either by not considering them for the analysis or replacing them with a suitable value.

To make this clearer, let's use a sample dataset to perform the various operations. We will use a dataset about India named `IndiaData`. You can find the dataset at `https://github.com/rsharankumar/R_Data_Science_Essentials`. We will perform preprocessing on the dataset:

```
data <- read.csv("IndiaData.csv", header = TRUE)
#1. To check the number of Null
sum(is.na(data))
[1] 6831
```

After reading the dataset, we use the `is.na` function to identify the presence of NA in the dataset, and then using `sum`, we get the total number of NAs present in the dataset. In our case, we can see that a large number of rows has NA in it. We can replace the NA with the mean value or we can remove these NA rows.

The following function can be used to replace the NA with the column mean for all the numeric columns. The numeric columns are identified by the `sapply(data, is.numeric)` function. We will check for the cells that have the NA value, then we identify the mean of these columns using the `mean` function with the `na.rm=TRUE` parameter, where the NA values are excluded while computing the `mean` function:

```
for (i in which(sapply(data, is.numeric))) {
  data[is.na(data[, i]), i] <- mean(data[, i],  na.rm = TRUE)
}
```

Alternatively, we can also remove all the NA rows from the dataset using the following code:

```
newdata <- na.omit(data)
```

The next major preprocessing activity is to identify the `outliers` package and deal with it. We can identify the presence of outliers in R by making use of the `outliers` function. We can use the function outliers only on the numeric columns, hence let's consider the preceding dataset, where the NAs were replaced by the mean values, and we will identify the presence of an outlier using the `outliers` function. Then, we get the location of all the outliers using the `which` function and finally, we remove the rows that had outlier values:

```
install.packages("outliers")
library(outliers)
```

We identify the outliers in the `X2012` column, which can be subsetted using the `data$X2012` command:

```
outlier_tf = outlier(data$X2012,logical=TRUE)
sum(outlier_tf)
[1] 1

#What were the outliers
find_outlier = which(outlier_tf==TRUE,arr.ind=TRUE)
#Removing the outliers
newdata = data[-find_outlier,]
nrow(newdata)
```

The column from the preceding dataset that was considered in the outlier example had only one outlier and hence we can remove this row from the dataset.

# Performing data operations

The following are the different data operations available in R:

- Arithmetic operations
- String operations
- Aggregation operations

# Arithmetic operations on the data

In this dataset, we will see the arithmetic operations performed on the data. We can perform various operations such as addition, subtraction, multiplication, division, exponentiation, and modulus. Let's see how these operations are performed in R. Let's first declare two numeric vectors:

```
a1 <- c(1,2,3,4,5)
b1 <- c(6,7,8,9,10)
c1 <- a1+b1
[1]   7   9 11 13 15
c1 <- b1-a1
 [1] 5 5 5 5 5
c1 <- b1*a1
 [1]   6  14  24  36  50
c1 <- b1/a1
 [1] 6.000000 3.500000 2.666667 2.250000 2.000000
```

Apart from those seen at the top, the other arithmetic operations are the exponentiation and modulus, which can be performed as follows, respectively:

```
c1 <- b1/a1
c1 <- b1 %% a1
```

Note that these aforementioned arithmetic operations can be performed between two or more numeric vectors of the same length.

We can also perform logical operations. In the following code, we will simply pass the values 1 to 10 to the dataset and then use the check condition to exclude the data based on the given condition. The condition actually returns the logical value; it checks all the values and returns TRUE when the condition is satisfied, or else, FALSE is returned.

```
x <- c(1:10)
x[(x>=8) | (x<=5)]
```

Having seen the various operations on variables, we will also check arithmetic operations on a matrix data. In the following code, we define two matrices that are exactly the same, and then multiply them. The resultant matrix is stored in newmat:

```
matdata1 <-matrix(1:25, nrow=5,ncol=5, dimnames=list(rnames, cnames))
matdata2 <-matrix(1:25, nrow=5,ncol=5, dimnames=list(rnames, cnames))
newmat <- matdata1 * matdata2
newmat
```

# String operations on the data

R supports a number of string operations. Many of these string operations are useful in data manipulation such as subsetting a string, replacing a string, changing the case, and splitting the string into characters. Now we will try each one of them in R.

The following code is used to get a part of the original string using the `substr` function; we need to pass the original string along with its starting location and the end location for the substring:

```
x <- "The Shawshank Redemption"
substr(x, 6, 14)
[1] "Shawshank"
```

The following code is used to search for a pattern in the character variables using the `grep` function, which searches for matches. In this function, we first pass the string that has to be found, then the second parameter will hold a vector; in this case, we specified a character vector, and the third parameter will say if the pattern is a string or regular expression. When `fixed=TRUE`, the pattern is a string, where as it is a regular expression if set as `FALSE`:

```
grep("Shawshank", c("The","Shawshank","Redemption"), fixed=TRUE)
 [1] 2
```

Now, we will see how to replace a character with another. In order to substitute a character with a new character, we use the `sub` function. In the following code, we replace the space with a semicolon. We pass three parameters to the following function. The first parameter will specify the string/character that has to be replaced, the second parameter tells us the new character/string, and finally, we pass the actual string:

```
sub("\\s",",","Hello There")
 [1] "Hello,There"
```

We can also split the string into characters. In order to perform this operation, we need to use the `strsplit` function. The following code will split the string into characters:

```
strsplit("Redemption", "")
 [1] "R" "e" "d" "e" "m" "p" "t" "i" "o" "n"
```

We have a `paste` function in R that will paste multiple strings or character variables. It is very useful when arriving at a string dynamically. This can be achieved using the following code:

```
paste("Today is", date())
[1] "Today is Fri Jun 26 01:39:26 2015"
```

In the preceding function, there is a space between the two strings. We can avoid this using a similar `paste0` function, which does the same operation but joins without any space. This function is very similar to the concatenation operation.

We can convert a string to uppercase or lowercase using the `toupper` and `tolower` functions.

# Aggregation operations on the data

We explored many of the arithmetic and string operations in R. Now, let's also have a look at the aggregation operation.

## Mean

For this exercise, let's consider the `mtcars` dataset in R. Read the dataset to a variable and then use the following code to calculate `mean` for a numeric column:

```
data <- mtcars
mean(data$mpg)
[1] 20.09062
```

## Median

The median can be obtained using the following code:

```
med <- median(data$mpg)
paste("Median MPG:", med)
[1] "Median MPG: 19.2"
```

## Sum

The `mtcars` dataset has details about various cars. Let's see what is the horsepower of all the cars in this dataset. We can calculate the sum using the following code:

```
hp <- sum(data$hp)
paste("Total HP:", hp)
[1] "Total HP: 4694"
```

## Maximum and minimum

The maximum value or minimum value can be found using the `max` and `min` functions. Look at the following code for reference:

```
max <- max(data$mpg)
min <- min(data$mpg)
paste("Maximum MPG:", max, "and Minimum MPG:", min)
[1] "Maximum MPG: 33.9 and Minimum MPG: 10.4"
```

## Standard deviation

We can calculate the standard deviation using the `sd` function. Look at the following code to get the standard deviation:

```
sd <- sd(data$mpg)
paste("Std Deviation of MPG:", sd)
[1] "Std Deviation of MPG: 6.0269480520891"
```

# Control structures in R

We have covered the different operations that are available in R. Now, let's look at the control structures used in R. Control structures are the key elements of any programming language.

The control structures commonly used in R are as follows:

- `if, else`: This is used to test a condition and execute based on the condition
- `for`: This is used to execute a loop for a fixed number of iterations
- `while`: This is used to execute a loop while a condition is true
- `repeat`: This is used to execute a loop indefinitely until seeking a break
- `break`: This is used to break the execution of a loop
- `next`: This is used to skip an iteration of a loop
- `return`: This is used to exit a function

# Control structures – if and else

The `if` and `else` control structures are used to execute based on a condition, where it performs the function when the condition is satisfied and performs an alternate function when the condition fails. (The else clause is not mandatory.) We can implement nested conditions as well in R.

```
if(<condition>) {
## do something
} else {
## do something else
}
```

# Control structures – for

The `for` loop is used to execute repetitive code statements for a definite number of iterations. The `for` loops are commonly used to iterate over the element of an object (list, vector, and so on).

```
for(i in 1:10) {
print(i)
}
```

# Control structures – while

The `while` loops are used to evaluate a condition repetitively. If the condition is true, then the expression in the loop body is executed until the condition becomes false.

```
count<-0
while(count<10) {
print(count)
count<-count+1
}
```

# Control structures – repeat and break

The `repeat` statement executes an expression in the loop repeatedly until it encounters a break.

The `break` statement can be used to terminate any loop. It is the only way to terminate a repeat loop.

```
> sum <- 1
> repeat
{
sum <- sum + 2;
print(sum);
if (sum > 11)
break;
}
3
5
7
9
11
13
```

# Control structures – next and return

The `next` control structure is used to skip a particular iteration in a loop based on a condition.

The `return` control structure signals that a function should exit a function and return a given value.

```
for(i in 1:5) {
if(i<=3) {
next
}
print(i)
}
[1] 4
[1] 5
```

# Bringing data to a usable format

We covered reading the data in R, understanding the data types, and performing various operations on the data. Now, we will see a few concepts that will be used just before an analysis or building a model. While performing an analysis, we might not need to study the entire dataset and we can just focus a subset of it, or, on the other hand, we might have to combine data from multiple data sources. These are the various concepts that will be covered in this chapter.

The most commonly used functionality will be to select the desired column from the dataset. While building the model, we will not be using all the columns in the dataset but just some of them that are more relevant. In order to select the column, we can either specify the column name or number, or simply delete the columns that are not required.

```
newdata <- data[c(1,5:10)]
head(newdata)
# excluding column
newdata <- data[c(-2, -3, -4, -11)]
head(newdata)
```

|                   | mpg  | drat | wt    | qsec  | vs | am | gear |
|-------------------|------|------|-------|-------|----|----|------|
| Mazda RX4         | 21.0 | 3.90 | 2.620 | 16.46 | 0  | 1  | 4    |
| Mazda RX4 Wag     | 21.0 | 3.90 | 2.875 | 17.02 | 0  | 1  | 4    |
| Datsun 710        | 22.8 | 3.85 | 2.320 | 18.61 | 1  | 1  | 4    |
| Hornet 4 Drive    | 21.4 | 3.08 | 3.215 | 19.44 | 1  | 0  | 3    |
| Hornet Sportabout | 18.7 | 3.15 | 3.440 | 17.02 | 0  | 0  | 3    |
| Valiant           | 18.1 | 2.76 | 3.460 | 20.22 | 1  | 0  | 3    |

In the preceding code, we first selected the column by its position. The first line of the code will select the first column and then the 5th to 10th column from the dataset, whereas, in the last line, the specified two columns are removed from the dataset. Both the preceding commands will yield the same result.

We can also arrive at a situation where we need to filter the data based on a condition. While building the model, we cannot create a single model for the whole of the population but we should create multiple models based on the behavior present in the population. This can be achieved by subsetting the dataset. In the following code, we will get the data of cars that have an mpg more than 25 alone:

```
newdata <- data[ which(data$mpg > 25), ]
```

|           | mpg  | cyl | disp | hp | drat | wt    | qsec  | vs | am | gear | carb |
|-----------|------|-----|------|----|------|-------|-------|----|----|------|------|
| Fiat 128  | 32.4 | 4   | 78.7 | 66 | 4.08 | 2.200 | 19.47 | 1  | 1  | 4    | 1    |

| | | | | | | | | | | |
|---|---|---|---|---|---|---|---|---|---|---|
| Honda Civic | 30.4 | 4 | 75.7 | 52 | 4.93 | 1.615 | 18.52 | 1 | 1 | 4 | 2 |
| Toyota Corolla | 33.9 | 4 | 71.1 | 65 | 4.22 | 1.835 | 19.90 | 1 | 1 | 4 | 1 |
| Fiat X1-9 | 27.3 | 4 | 79.0 | 66 | 4.08 | 1.935 | 18.90 | 1 | 1 | 4 | 1 |
| Porsche 914-2 | 26.0 | 4 | 120.3 | 91 | 4.43 | 2.140 | 16.70 | 0 | 1 | 5 | 2 |
| Lotus Europa | 30.4 | 4 | 95.1 | 113 | 3.77 | 1.513 | 16.90 | 1 | 1 | 5 | 2 |

We might also need to consider a sample of the dataset. For example, while building a regression or logistic model, we need to have two datasets—one for the training and the other for the testing. In these cases, we need to choose a random sample. This can be done using the following code:

```
sample <- data[sample(1:nrow(data), 10, replace=FALSE),]
sample
```

| | mpg | cyl | disp | hp | drat | wt | qsec | vs | am | gear | carb |
|---|---|---|---|---|---|---|---|---|---|---|---|
| Honda Civic | 30.4 | 4 | 75.7 | 52 | 4.93 | 1.615 | 18.52 | 1 | 1 | 4 | 2 |
| Porsche 914-2 | 26.0 | 4 | 120.3 | 91 | 4.43 | 2.140 | 16.70 | 0 | 1 | 5 | 2 |
| Merc 450SLC | 15.2 | 8 | 275.8 | 180 | 3.07 | 3.780 | 18.00 | 0 | 0 | 3 | 3 |
| Dodge Challenger | 15.5 | 8 | 318.0 | 150 | 2.76 | 3.520 | 16.87 | 0 | 0 | 3 | 2 |
| Duster 360 | 14.3 | 8 | 360.0 | 245 | 3.21 | 3.570 | 15.84 | 0 | 0 | 3 | 4 |
| Fiat X1-9 | 27.3 | 4 | 79.0 | 66 | 4.08 | 1.935 | 18.90 | 1 | 1 | 4 | 1 |
| Fiat 128 | 32.4 | 4 | 78.7 | 66 | 4.08 | 2.200 | 19.47 | 1 | 1 | 4 | 1 |
| Lotus Europa | 30.4 | 4 | 95.1 | 113 | 3.77 | 1.513 | 16.90 | 1 | 1 | 5 | 2 |
| Toyota Corona | 21.5 | 4 | 120.1 | 97 | 3.70 | 2.465 | 20.01 | 1 | 0 | 3 | 1 |
| Mazda RX4 Wag | 21.0 | 6 | 160.0 | 110 | 3.90 | 2.875 | 17.02 | 0 | 1 | 4 | 4 |

We considered a random sample of 10 rows from the dataset. Along with these, we might have to merge two different datasets. Let's see how this can be achieved. We can combine the data both row-wise as well as column-wise as follows:

```
sample1 <- data[sample(1:nrow(data), 10, replace=FALSE),]
sample2 <- data[sample(1:nrow(data), 5, replace=FALSE),]
newdata <- rbind(sample1, sample2)
```

The preceding code is used to combine two datasets that share the same column format. Then we can combine them using the rbind function. Alternatively, if the two datasets have the same length of data but different columns, then we can combine them using the cind or merge functions:

```
newdata1 <- data[c(1,5:7)]
newdata2 <- data[c(8:11)]
newdata <- cbind(newdata1, newdata2)
```

When we have two different datasets with a common column, then we can use the `merge` function to combine them. On using `merge`, the dataset will be merged based on the common columns.

These are the essential concepts necessary to prepare the dataset for the analysis, which will be discussed in the next few chapters.

# Summary

In this chapter, you learned to import and read data from different sources such as CSV, TXT, XLSX, and relational data sources and the different data types available in R such as numeric, integer, character, and logical data types. We covered the basic data preprocessing techniques used to handle outliers, missing data, and inconsistencies in order to facilitate analysis.

You learned to perform different arithmetic operations that can be performed on the data using R, such as addition, subtraction, multiplication, division, exponentiation, and modulus, and also learned the string operations that can be performed on the data using R, such as subsetting a string, replacing a string, changing the case, and splitting the string into characters, which helps in data manipulation. Finally, you learned about the different control structures in R, such as `if`, `else`, `for`, `while`, `repeat`, `break`, `next`, and `return`, which facilitate a recursive or logical execution. We also covered bringing data to a usable format for analysis and building a model. In the next chapter, we will see how to perform exploratory data analysis using R. It will include a few statistical techniques and also variable analyses, such as univariate, bivariate, and multivariate analyses.

# 2

# Exploratory Data Analysis

Exploratory data analysis is a very important topic in the field of data analysis. It is an approach of analyzing the data and summarizing the main characteristics of the dataset. The main objective of exploratory data analysis is to check various hypotheses in order to get a better understanding about the dataset.

Exploratory data analysis includes many statistical techniques and visual and nonvisual analysis. When your study has to be communicated with peers as well as with other audience with non-data science backgrounds, it is advisable to use a lot of visual techniques that help in better communications.

Some of the expectations out of exploratory data analysis are getting insights out of the data, extracting the important variables in the dataset (depending on the problem to be solved), identifying the outliers in the data, and getting results of various testing hypotheses. These results play a very important role in how to solve the business problems, and if it is a modeling problem, then deciding on which model to use and how to apply it to the dataset for enhanced accuracy.

In this chapter, you will learn how to perform exploratory data analysis starting with getting a generalized view on the data, analysis of one variable at a time, then bi-variable analysis, and finally, analyzing multiple variables to get a better understanding on interdependencies.

The topics that will be covered in this chapter are as follows:

- Titanic dataset
- Descriptive statistics
- Inferential statistics
- Univariate analysis
- Bivariate analysis
- Multivariate analysis (scatter plot with segments, heatmap, and tabulation)

# The Titanic dataset

In this chapter, let's use the Titanic dataset, which is available on the Internet and also hosted on **GitHub,** to implement various techniques. Place the dataset in the current working directory in R; before this, first set the working directory accordingly using the `setwd()` command. The `setwd()` function is used to specify the location that should be considered as the current working directory. Now, read the data using the `read.csv` function and store it in a data frame. In this book, we have named the data frame `tdata`. The various details that are present in the dataset, which is hosted on GitHub, are as follows:

```
tdata<- read.csv("titanic.csv")

names(tdata)
```

The output of the preceding command is as follows:

```
> names(tdata)
 [1] "PassengerId" "Survived"   "Pclass"    "Name"     "Sex"
 [6] "Age"         "Sibsp"      "Parch"     "Ticket"   "Fare"
[11] "Cabin"       "Embarked"
```

These are the various columns captured in the dataset. The explanation of these variables is given. For more detailed understanding about the dataset, visit `https://www.kaggle.com/c/titanic/data`. We have used the file named `train.csv` for our learning purpose.

The variable description is as follows:

| Variable | Description |
|----------|-------------|
| Survival | Survival (0 = No; 1 = Yes) |
| Pclass | Passenger class (1 = 1st; 2 = 2nd; 3 = 3rd) |
| Name | Name |
| Sex | Sex |
| Age | Age |
| Sibsp | Number of siblings/spouses aboard |
| Parch | Number of parents/children aboard |
| Ticket | Ticket number |
| Fare | Passenger fare |
| Cabin | Cabin |
| Embarked | Port of embarkation (C = Cherbourg; Q = Queenstown; S = Southampton) |

The snapshot of the preceding dataset is shown here using the `head` function:

**head(tdata)**

```
> head(tdata)
  PassengerId Survived Pclass                                                Name    Sex Age
1           1        0      3                             Braund, Mr. Owen Harris   male  22
2           2        1      1 Cumings, Mrs. John Bradley (Florence Briggs Thayer) female  38
3           3        1      3                              Heikkinen, Miss. Laina female  26
4           4        1      1       Futrelle, Mrs. Jacques Heath (Lily May Peel) female  35
5           5        0      3                            Allen, Mr. William Henry   male  35
6           6        0      3                                    Moran, Mr. James   male  NA
  SibSp Parch          Ticket    Fare Cabin Embarked
1     1     0       A/5 21171  7.2500              S
2     1     0        PC 17599 71.2833   C85        C
3     0     0 STON/O2. 3101282  7.9250              S
4     1     0          113803 53.1000  C123        S
5     0     0          373450  8.0500              S
6     0     0          330877  8.4583              Q
```

# Descriptive statistics

Descriptive statistics is a method of summarizing a dataset quantitatively. These summaries can be simple quantitative statements about the data or a visual representation sufficient enough to be part of the initial description about the dataset.

To get a basic understanding about the dataset, we can use the built-in function `summary`. This function quickly scans the dataset and provides the following information about the dataset. This will really help in getting a first-cut understanding about the data. This will be useful for numerical as well as categorical data.

**summary(tdata)**

The output is as follows:

```
> summary(tdata)
  PassengerId          Survived            Pclass
 Min.   :  1.0    Min.   :0.0000    Min.   :1.000
 1st Qu.:223.5    1st Qu.:0.0000    1st Qu.:2.000
 Median :446.0    Median :0.0000    Median :3.000
 Mean   :446.0    Mean   :0.3838    Mean   :2.309
 3rd Qu.:668.5    3rd Qu.:1.0000    3rd Qu.:3.000
 Max.   :891.0    Max.   :1.0000    Max.   :3.000

                                      Name           Sex           Age
 Abbing, Mr. Anthony                  :  1    female:314    Min.   : 0.42
 Abbott, Mr. Rossmore Edward          :  1    male  :577    1st Qu.:20.12
 Abbott, Mrs. Stanton (Rosa Hunt)     :  1                  Median :28.00
 Abelson, Mr. Samuel                  :  1                  Mean   :29.70
 Abelson, Mrs. Samuel (Hannah wizosky):  1                  3rd Qu.:38.00
 Adahl, Mr. Mauritz Nils Martin       :  1                  Max.   :80.00
 (Other)                              :885                  NA's   :177
     SibSp            Parch             Ticket           Fare
 Min.   :0.000    Min.   :0.0000    1601    :  7    Min.   :  0.00
 1st Qu.:0.000    1st Qu.:0.0000    347082  :  7    1st Qu.:  7.91
 Median :0.000    Median :0.0000    CA. 2343:  7    Median : 14.45
 Mean   :0.523    Mean   :0.3816    3101295 :  6    Mean   : 32.20
 3rd Qu.:1.000    3rd Qu.:0.0000    347088  :  6    3rd Qu.: 31.00
 Max.   :8.000    Max.   :6.0000    CA 2144 :  6    Max.   :512.33
                                    (Other) :852
          Cabin         Embarked
             :687        :  2
 B96 B98     :  4    C:168
 C23 C25 C27:  4    Q: 77
 G6          :  4    S:644
 C22 C26     :  3
 D           :  3
 (Other)     :186
```

The summary function provides us with a high-level detail about the variables in the dataset. In order to know more about the dataset such as the missing values, distribution of numerical variables, and distinct values of categorical variables, we need to use an additional package called Hmisc. (The implementation of this is given here.) The package can be installed using the install.packages function and loaded to the R environment using the library function. Then, using the function described here, we get the desired output:

```
install.packages("Hmisc")
library(Hmisc)
describe(tdata)
```

The output of the preceding command is as follows:

```
Survived
      n missing unique    Info    Sum    Mean
    891       0      2    0.71    342  0.3838
-------------------------------------------------------------------------------
Pclass
      n missing unique    Info    Mean
    891       0      3    0.81   2.309

1 (216, 24%), 2 (184, 21%), 3 (491, 55%)
-------------------------------------------------------------------------------
Name
      n missing unique
    891       0    891

lowest : Abbing, Mr. Anthony                  Abbott, Mr. Rossmore Edward        Abbott, Mrs. Stanton (Rosa Hunt)
belson, Mr. Samuel                      Abelson, Mrs. Samuel (Hannah Wizosky)
highest: Youssef, Mr. Gerious               Yrois, Miss. Henriette ("Mrs Harbeck") Zabour, Miss. Hileni
abour, Miss. Thamine                    Zimmerman, Mr. Leo
-------------------------------------------------------------------------------
Sex
      n missing unique
    891       0      2

female (314, 35%), male (577, 65%)
-------------------------------------------------------------------------------
Age
      n missing unique    Info    Mean    .05    .10    .25    .50    .75    .90    .95
    714     177     88       1    29.7   4.00  14.00  20.12  28.00  38.00  50.00  56.00

lowest :  0.42  0.67  0.75  0.83  0.92, highest: 70.00 70.50 71.00 74.00 80.00
-------------------------------------------------------------------------------
SibSp
      n missing unique    Info    Mean
    891       0      7    0.67   0.523

                0   1  2  3  4 5 8
Frequency 608 209 28 16 18 5 7
%               68  23  3  2  2 1 1
-------------------------------------------------------------------------------
```

There are a few more functions in R that will be useful for the summary analysis, which can be applied to the variables individually. To get to know the standard deviation of the dataset, we can use the `sd` function that can be applied to the numerical variables only:

```
sd(tdata$Fare)
```

The output of the preceding command is as follows:

```
[1] 49.69343
```

To get the details about the percentile, we can use the `quantile` function. Let's try to use the `quantile` function on the `Fare` variable and check the distribution:

```
quantile(tdata$Fare)
```

The output of the preceding command is as follows:

```
> quantile(tdata$Fare)
      0%      25%      50%      75%     100%
  0.0000   7.9104  14.4542  31.0000 512.3292
```

By default, we get the percentile at an interval of 0.25 only, but we can change this using the `probs` parameter. We will try the same thing but with an interval of ten percentile:

```
quantile(tdata$Fare, probs = seq(0, 1, 0.1))
```

The following is the output of the preceding command:

```
> quantile(tdata$Fare, probs = seq(0, 1, 0.1))
      0%      10%      20%      30%      40%      50%      60%      70%
  0.0000   7.5500   7.8542   8.0500  10.5000  14.4542  21.6792  27.0000
     80%      90%     100%
 39.6875  77.9583 512.3292
```

These are the some of the basic descriptive statistics techniques. These techniques are sufficient to get the first opinion about the dataset.

# Box plot

We can represent the data presented by `summary` in a graphical format using the `boxplot` function. The box plot can be plotted for the numerical columns only; hence, we first select the numerical columns and then use the `boxplot` function to plot it. This box plot shows the median, first quartile, and third quartile values for all the variables. The outliers can also be shown in the dataset. In the following boxplot, the outliers have been disabled:

```
bplot<- tdata[c("Pclass", "Age", "SibSp", "Parch", "Fare", "Cabin")]
boxplot(bplot, outline = FALSE)
```

The output of the preceding command is as follows:

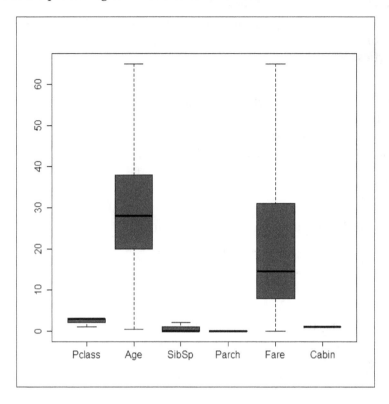

# Exercise

We have so far performed descriptive statistical analysis on the Titanic dataset. After trying out the preceding example, download a public dataset and try out the techniques that you have learned.

The public dataset can be accessed from the following links:

- http://www.google.com/publicdata/directory
- http://www.scaleunlimited.com/datasets/public-datasets/
- http://www.kdnuggets.com/2011/02/free-public-datasets.html

# Inferential statistics

We have seen a sufficient number of descriptive statistics techniques. Now, let's check some of the inferential statistics techniques. Inferential statistics is used to infer properties about the dataset.

First, let's start with the simple mean and check what should be the range if the mean has to fall under the confidence interval of 95%. In order to get the confidence interval for the mean, we need to load the lsr package; if the package is not already installed, you need to install it using the install.packages function and then the ciMean function to get the desired result:

```
library(lsr)
```

```
ciMean(tdata$Fare)
```

The following is the output of the preceding command:

```
> ciMean(tdata$Fare)
            2.5%     97.5%
[1,] 28.93683 35.47158
```

The ciMean function gives us an overall view on the confidence interval of the Fare variable. However, to see how different it is between male and female, we can use the aggregate function:

```
aggregate( tdata$Fare ~ tdata$Sex, tdata, ciMean )
```

The output of the preceding is as follows:

```
> aggregate( tdata$Fare ~ tdata$Sex, tdata, ciMean )
  tdata$Sex tdata$Fare.1 tdata$Fare.2
1    female     38.03996     50.91968
2      male     21.99664     29.05114
```

From the preceding output, we can infer that the mean fare for male was quite less compared to that of the female passengers. Additionally, we get to know that the range for the female passengers is quite large compared to the male passengers.

Now, let's perform t-test to get to know about the interval estimate of the difference in the population mean of two different independent data samples assuming that the dataset follows a normal distribution. We will use the Titanic dataset and consider the Sex column to divide the dataset into two different independent samples:

```
t.test( tdata$Fare ~ tdata$Sex, data = tdata )
```

The following is the output of the preceding command:

```
welch Two Sample t-test

data:  tdata$Fare by tdata$Sex
t = 5.0775, df = 504.964, p-value = 5.388e-07
alternative hypothesis: true difference in means is not equal to 0
95 percent confidence interval:
 11.62117 26.29068
sample estimates:
mean in group female    mean in group male
         44.47982                25.52389
```

From the preceding example, the mean fare for the female passengers was `44.47982` and the mean fare for the male passengers was `25.52389`. At a 95% confidence interval, the difference in the mean fare of the female passengers with that of the male passengers was in the range of 11.62117 to 26.29068.

Let's understand if two variables are related to each other or not. We will consider the age and fare and find the correlation between them. We can find the correlation using the `cor` function:

```
cor(tdata$Fare, tdata$Age, use="complete")
```

```
[1] 0.09606669
```

We got the correlation between the `Age` and `Fare` variables. In order to get the range of the correlation with the confidence interval set at 95%, we need to use the `corr` function:

```
cor.test(tdata$Fare, tdata$Age, use="complete")
```

The output of the preceding command is as follows:

```
> cor.test(tdata$Fare, tdata$Age, use="complete")

 Pearson's product-moment correlation

data:  tdata$Fare and tdata$Age
t = 2.5753, df = 712, p-value = 0.01022
alternative hypothesis: true correlation is not equal to 0
95 percent confidence interval:
 0.02285549 0.16825304
sample estimates:
      cor
0.09606669
```

From the preceding output, we get to know about the range of correlation at the confidence interval range of 95%. The correlation ranges from 0.023 as well as 0.168. These are some of the basic statistical techniques that are generally used to infer details from a large amount of data.

# Univariate analysis

Univariate analysis is the simplest form of analysis, where we consider only one variable at a time and understand the data. Some of the measures have already been covered in descriptive statistics such as the mean and median of the data.

We will perform one more univariate analysis: the distribution of the data. We will consider the age of the people who had travelled in the Titanic, and we will find out how many people were there in the different age groups:

```
age <- na.omit(tdata$Age)
```

First, we read the data to the `age` data frame by excluding the cases where the age was not present. As we want to get the distribution on a fixed range, we first get the age of the youngest as well as the oldest person who travelled on the ship from the available dataset using the `seq` function. We set the starting value as 0 and the last value as 80; we also set the interval as 10:

```
range(age)
breaks = seq(0, 80, by=10)
```

We created the intervals and stored them in the variable breaks. Using the `cut` function, we can classify the people into different age groups as per the definition in the `breaks` variable:

```
ageBreak = cut(age, breaks, right=FALSE)
```

We use the `table` function to find the frequency distribution of the `age` variable. We can then convert the data format into a data frame for the ease of readability:

```
ageDistribution = table(ageBreak)
ageDistribution<- data.frame(ageDistribution)
data.frame(ageDistribution)
```

The output of the preceding command is as follows:

```
> data.frame(ageDistribution)
  ageBreak Freq
1   [0,10)   62
2  [10,20)  102
3  [20,30)  220
4  [30,40)  167
5  [40,50)   89
6  [50,60)   48
7  [60,70)   19
8  [70,80)    6
```

This is a tabular representation of the data; we can also represent the same data in a graphical format for an easy understanding as well as a good grasp. We need to use the ggplot2 package to plot attractive graphs in R, but as mentioned previously, ensure that the package is installed first. We use the colnames function to give suitable names to the columns of the preceding table:

```
library(ggplot2)
colnames(ageDistribution) <- c("Range","No.Of.People")
```

We then use the qplot function to draw the histogram for the frequency distribution. Along with the data points, we also pass a few more parameters to make sure that the graph looks good and the data presented is easy to read. We use the geom_bar parameter to pass the color of the graph, and finally, we save the plot using the ggsave function:

```
q <- qplot(x=Range, y=No.Of.People,
data=ageDistribution, geom="bar", stat="identity",
position="dodge")
q + geom_bar(stat="identity", fill="#0000FF", colour="black")
```

The following is the output of the preceding code:

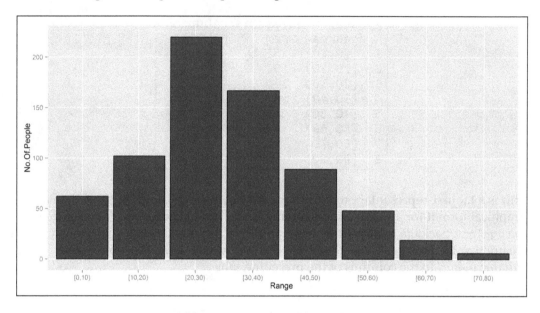

```
ggsave(file="Distribution.png", dpi=500)
```

The preceding command will help save the output to the local system.

We will now explore the gender of the passengers who travelled in the Titanic. We can get the count easily through the summary function, but we will plot this using a pie chart:

```
pieChart<- ggplot(tdata, aes(x = factor(1), fill = factor(tdata$Sex))) +
geom_bar(width = 1)

pieChart + coord_polar(theta = "y") +

ggtitle("Male and female")
```

The output of the preceding code snippet is as follows:

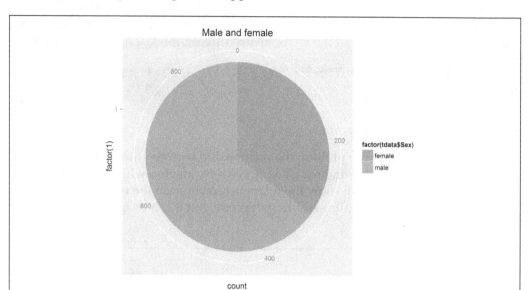

Similar to the previous examples, we used a few parameters here along with the data for a better output. We will use the `ggtitle` parameter to give a heading for this chart. We will use the `coord_polar` parameter to indicate that the plot should be a pie chart, and finally, we will save the file using the `ggsave` function:

```
ggsave(file="pie-chart-sex.png", dpi=500)
```

These are some of the univariate analysis examples that can be performed on the dataset. These graphical outputs help us grasp the results easily. These techniques will be really useful while making business presentations.

# Bivariate analysis

In this section, we will cover bivariate analysis to understand the combined effect of two variables as well as the effect of one variable on the other variable. In any real-life example, there will be multiple variables dependent on each other. Hence, this analysis will be useful in getting an understanding about these cases.

The best method to get a quick understanding about two variables is the scatter plot. This visual representation gives us a clear idea about the impact of one variable on the other variable. We can use the same `ggplot` function to plot the scatter plot. We will plot the scatter chart to get the relationship between the `Age` and `Fare` variables:

```
ggplot(tdata, aes(x=Fare, y=Age)) +
geom_point(shape=1) +
geom_smooth(method=lm)
ggsave(file="scatter-plot.png", dpi=500)
```

In the preceding case, we are plotting the relationship between these two variables along with the scatter plot, using the `geom_smooth` parameter, which plots an additional linear line that will show the relationship between the two variables. There might be a warning while executing the code, but it can be ignored. The output will look as follows:

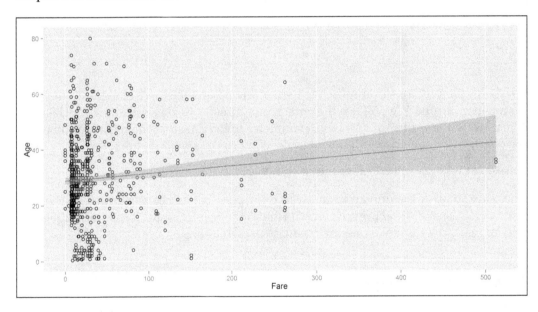

From the preceding graph, it is very clear that the variables have a positive relationship, that is, when **Age** of the passenger increases, **Fare** tends to increase. Additionally, we can see that the concentration of the fare toward the lower side is very high compared to the high-value fares, whereas the age has a normal distribution.

Thus, we got the relationship between the two variables. The preceding method provides us with a qualitative measure, but we still don't have a clear idea on what is the most likely increase in **Fare** of the passenger when **Age** of the passenger increases by $x$ units. We can get the quantitative measure using the correlation function as follows:

```
cor(tdata$Age, tdata$Fare, use= "pairwise.complete.obs")
  [1] 0.09606669
```

In the preceding function, we used the `use` parameter and set it to `pairwise.complete.obs` to make sure that we consider the rows where values of both the columns are present while computing the correlation; otherwise, we might end up with a wrong correlation value.

Though visual representation would be the best way to communicate, the cross-tabulation analysis methods are the best to dig deep into the dataset. Usually, in any analysis, cross-tabulations are extensively used to get insights from the data.

We can perform cross-tabulation analysis using the `xtabs` function. We will consider the variables for `Survived` and `Sex` and get the `data` in the table format using the `ftable` function:

```
tab<-xtabs(~Survived+Sex, data=tdata)
ftable(tab)
```

The output of the preceding command is as follows:

```
> ftable(tab)
            Sex female male
Survived
0                   81  468
1                  233  109
```

In the preceding case, we get the actual number, but it will be easy to understand the impact if the same data had been presented in percentages, which can be achieved using the following code:

```
result <- replace(tab, , sprintf("%.1f%%",prop.table(tab,2)*100))
```

The output of the preceding command is as follows:

```
> result
           Sex
Survived female  male
       0  25.8%  81.1%
       1  74.2%  18.9%
```

Cross-tabulation analysis is very powerful. When used extensively on the various variables in the dataset, we can get a very good understanding of the data. In most cases, cross-tabulations are used to explore the patterns and, once found, they are represented in a suitable graph for easy communication.

# Multivariate analysis

In the case of multivariate analysis, we consider more than two variables for the study. The general approach is to perform single variable analysis and then, double variable analysis, and, finally, consider the significant one for multivariate analysis.

# Cross-tabulation analysis

Let's first perform cross-tabulation with three variables. It is very similar to the two-variable cross-tabulation analysis but, instead of just two variables, we pass three variables here. Using the `ftable` function, we can see the tabular data:

```
tab<-xtabs(~Survived+Sex+SibSp, data=tdata)
```

```
ftable(tab)
```

The output of the preceding command is as follows:

```
> ftable(tab)
                SibSp    0    1    2    3    4    5    8
Survived Sex
0        female           37   26    3    7    4    1    3
         male            361   71   12    5   11    4    4
1        female          137   80   10    4    2    0    0
         male             73   32    3    0    1    0    0
```

In order to get the details in percentages, we can use the following code. As there are three variables, we need to specify the column on which the percentage has to be computed. In the following code, we specify `prop.table(tab, 3)`, which means that the percentages will be computed based on the third column, `SibSp`:

```
result <- replace(tab, , sprintf("%.1f%%",prop.table(tab,3)*100))
data.frame(result)
```

The following is the output:

```
> data.frame(result)
   Survived    Sex SibSp  Freq
1         0 female     0  6.1%
2         1 female     0 22.5%
3         0   male     0 59.4%
4         1   male     0 12.0%
5         0 female     1 12.4%
6         1 female     1 38.3%
7         0   male     1 34.0%
8         1   male     1 15.3%
9         0 female     2 10.7%
10        1 female     2 35.7%
11        0   male     2 42.9%
12        1   male     2 10.7%
13        0 female     3 43.8%
14        1 female     3 25.0%
15        0   male     3 31.2%
16        1   male     3  0.0%
17        0 female     4 22.2%
18        1 female     4 11.1%
19        0   male     4 61.1%
20        1   male     4  5.6%
21        0 female     5 20.0%
22        1 female     5  0.0%
23        0   male     5 80.0%
24        1   male     5  0.0%
25        0 female     8 42.9%
26        1 female     8  0.0%
27        0   male     8 57.1%
28        1   male     8  0.0%
```

We will also explore some of the graphical representations in multivariate analysis.

# Graphical analysis

We can check the trend of multiple variables. In the following example, we will compare three variables at a time. We will plot the survival and non-survival along with the age and measure the impact. We need to use the `sqldf` package so that we can format the data as per our requirement by writing the SQL queries. Before loading the package in the R environment, always ensure that you install the package and its dependencies:

```
library(sqldf)
trendData1<- sqldf("select Age, count(PassengerId) from tdata where
Survived in ('1') group by Age")
colnames(trendData1) <- c("Age","Survived")
trendData2<- sqldf("select Age, count(PassengerId) from tdata where
Survived in ('0') group by Age")
colnames(trendData2) <- c("Age","NotSurvived")
trendData<- sqldf("select a.Age, Survived, NotSurvived from trendData1 a
inner join trendData2 b on a.Age = b.Age")
head(trendData)
```

The output of the preceding command is as follows:

```
> head(trendData)
  Age Survived NotSurvived
1   1        5           2
2   2        3           7
3   3        5           1
4   4        7           3
5   6        2           1
6   7        1           2
```

The code that we have written formats the data to the preceding format. We have done a group by `Age` to make sure that there is no duplication in `Age` so that we can plot the line chart. The following code is then used to reformat the data so that we can use just one plot for this multiseries line chart:

```
library(reshape)
combinedData<- melt(trendData, id = 'Age')
ggplot(combinedData, aes(x = Age, y = value, colour = variable)) +
geom_line() +
ylab(label="Survival and Death") +
xlab("Age of the passenger") +
scale_colour_manual(values=c("green", "red"))
```

The output of the preceding command is as follows:

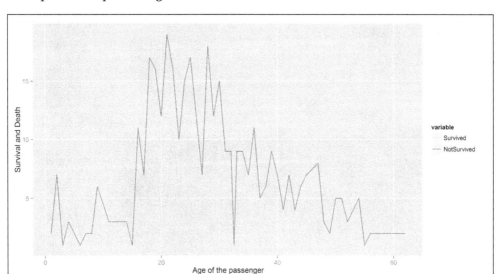

In the preceding plot, the red line represents the number of people who died, and the green line represents the number of people who survived. We can infer that the people between the ages of 20 and 30 had a low probability of survival.

# Summary

In this chapter, we covered how to implement various exploratory data analysis techniques using the Titanic dataset. Additionally, you learned descriptive statistics to summarize the dataset quantitatively as simple quantitative statements or as a visual representation using the summary function as well as the box plots. Moreover, we covered inferential statistics to infer the properties of the dataset that are of interest. Further, you also learned about univariate analysis, where the analysis is done using only one variable at a time to understand the data, and bivariate analysis, where the analysis is done using two variables to understand the data. The effect of one variable over the other was also covered. Finally, we explored multivariate analysis by considering more than two variables for the study by performing single variable analysis and then, double variable analysis, and finally, we considered the significant one for multivariate analysis using the scatter plot with segments, heatmap, and tabulations.

In the next chapter, you will be introduced to the different techniques to extract patterns from the raw data as well as derive sequential patterns hidden in the data. We will also touch on the evaluation metrics and how they can be adjusted to rank order the association rules. We will also discuss business cases where these techniques can be used.

# 3
# Pattern Discovery

Pattern discovery is an important concept in the field of data science. The ability to recognize a pattern is a very essential skill set for a data science professional to make accurate decisions. Though the pattern discovery skill generally comes with past experience, common sense, and intuition, there are also ways to extract it from the dataset.

The simplest way to know about the patterns in the dataset would be to visualize the data and look out for patterns in it. This method is very appropriate for the time series data to know about the seasonality and trends hidden in it.

As we have already covered visualizing data in R in the previous chapter, we will focus only on learning affinity analysis, which looks out for the co-occurrence of events in the dataset that would be impossible to know from just visualizing the data or browsing through it. Additionally, we will study about the sequence analysis where we will analyze various sequences of events and understand which event might lead to a certain consequence.

The objective of this chapter is to learn how to extract patterns in the dataset and hence, make predictions on an event occurrence well before time. For example, manufacturing companies can predict failures well before time using the extracted patterns and be equipped with the mitigation plans.

The topics that will be covered in this chapter are as follows:

- Transactional datasets
- **Apriori** analysis
- Support, confidence, and lift
- Filtering rules generated
- Plotting
- Sequential datasets

- Apriori sequence analysis
- Understanding the results
- Use cases for exercise

# Transactional datasets

Before going into the details of affinity analysis, we will first understand the types of datasets that will be used for the affinity analysis to extract patterns on the co-occurrence of events.

# Using the built-in dataset

First, let's understand the built-in AdultUCI dataset, which comes with the arules package. The data is in the data frame format, so we will see how to convert this into a transactional dataset:

```
library(arules)
```

This package is required in order to perform affinity analysis using R. Now, let's load the dataset that comes along with this package:

```
data("AdultUCI")
class(AdultUCI)
[1] "data.frame"
```

As you can see in the preceding output, the dataset is in the format of a data frame. We need to convert the AdultUCI dataset into a transactional dataset. Before converting, we will see the attributes present in the dataset using the head function, which will display the top five rows by default:

```
head(AdultUCI)
```

The output of the preceding command is as follows:

```
> head(AdultUCI)
  age           workclass fnlwgt education education-num
1  39           State-gov  77516 Bachelors            13
2  50   Self-emp-not-inc  83311 Bachelors            13
3  38             Private 215646   HS-grad             9
4  53             Private 234721      11th             7
5  28             Private 338409 Bachelors            13
6  37             Private 284582   Masters            14
      marital-status          occupation  relationship  race    sex
1      Never-married        Adm-clerical Not-in-family white   Male
2 Married-civ-spouse     Exec-managerial       Husband white   Male
3           Divorced   Handlers-cleaners Not-in-family white   Male
4 Married-civ-spouse   Handlers-cleaners       Husband Black   Male
5 Married-civ-spouse       Prof-specialty          Wife Black Female
6 Married-civ-spouse     Exec-managerial          Wife white Female
  capital-gain capital-loss hours-per-week native-country income
1         2174            0             40  United-States  small
2            0            0             13  United-States  small
3            0            0             40  United-States  small
4            0            0             40  United-States  small
5            0            0             40           Cuba  small
6            0            0             40  United-States  small
```

In the preceding dataset, we will remove the columns that have numerical values and retain only the columns with the categorical values as the pattern discovery using Apriori works best with a categorical dataset:

```
AdultUCI[["fnlwgt"]] <- NULL
```

```
AdultUCI[["education-num"]] <- NULL
```

Now, we convert the other attributes into categorical values. In the following code, we split the defined range of values as per the labels mentioned in the code. Similarly, we convert the other columns into categories, as shown in the following code:

```
AdultUCI[[ "age"]] <- ordered(cut(AdultUCI[[ "age"]],
c(15,25,45,65,100)), labels = c("Young", "Middle-aged", "Senior", "Old"))
```

```
AdultUCI[[ "hours-per-week"]] <- ordered(cut(AdultUCI[[ "hours-per-
week"]], c(0,25,40,60,168)), labels = c("Part-time", "Full-time", "Over-
time", "Workaholic"))
```

```
AdultUCI[[ "capital-gain"]] <- ordered(cut(AdultUCI[[ "capital-gain"]],
c(-Inf,0,median(AdultUCI[[ "capital-gain"]][AdultUCI[[ "capital-
gain"]]>0]), Inf)), labels = c("None", "Low", "High"))
```

```
AdultUCI[[ "capital-loss"]] <- ordered(cut(AdultUCI[[ "capital-loss"]],
c(-Inf,0, median(AdultUCI[[ "capital-loss"]][AdultUCI[[ "capital-
loss"]]>0]), Inf)), labels = c("None", "Low", "High"))
```

The preceding code will create additional categorical columns in the dataset. Using the following code, we can convert the data in the form of a data frame into a transactional dataset:

```
Adult <- as(AdultUCI, "transactions")
```

This can also be found in the document pertaining to the `arules` package. We can directly use the `Adult` dataset, which would hold the processed transactional data, but, for better understanding purposes, we convert the data frame into the required format:

```
class(Adult)
[1] "transactions"
attr(,"package")
[1] "arules"
```

Thus, we have converted the dataset into the transactional format. In order to get an outlook of the data, we can use the `summary` function. Here, we can see the output of the function that shows us the number of transactions, items, average number of items per transaction, and so on:

```
summary(Adult)
```

The output of the preceding command is as follows:

```
> summary(Adult)
transactions as itemMatrix in sparse format with
 48842 rows (elements/itemsets/transactions) and
 115 columns (items) and a density of 0.1089939

most frequent items:
          capital-loss=None                    capital-gain=None
                    46560                                  44807
native-country=United-States                        race=white
                    43832                                  41762
          workclass=Private                              (Other)
                    33906                                 401333

element (itemset/transaction) length distribution:
sizes
    9     10    11    12    13
   19    971  2067 15623 30162

   Min. 1st Qu.  Median    Mean 3rd Qu.    Max.
   9.00   12.00   13.00   12.53   13.00   13.00

includes extended item information - examples:
          labels variables       levels
1       age=Young       age        Young
2 age=Middle-aged       age  Middle-aged
3      age=Senior       age       Senior

includes extended transaction information - examples:
   transactionID
1              1
2              2
3              3
```

We can also take a look at the structure of the dataset by converting it into a data frame format and visualizing it. We use the following code and convert it into a data frame format so that we can visualize the dataset. The purpose of the conversion will be understood after viewing the transactional data in the data frame format.

```
Adultdf<- as(Adult, "data.frame")
```

```
head(Adultdf, 2)
```

The following is the output of the preceding command:

```
> head(Adultdf, 2)

                          items
1       {age=Middle-aged,workclass=State-gov,education=Bachelors,marital-status=Never-married,occupation=Adm-clerica
l,relationship=Not-in-family,race=white,sex=Male,capital-gain=Low,capital-loss=None,hours-per-week=Full-time,native
-country=United-States,income=small}
2 {age=Senior,workclass=Self-emp-not-inc,education=Bachelors,marital-status=Married-civ-spouse,occupation=Exec-mana
gerial,relationship=Husband,race=white,sex=Male,capital-gain=None,capital-loss=None,hours-per-week=Part-time,native
-country=United-States,income=small}
  transactionID
1             1
2             2
```

This dataset is ready for the application of the apriori algorithm and rule generation. Having seen how to convert a normal dataset with categorical/bucketed (after processing) columns into a transactional dataset, we can now understand a similar dataset by preparing it ourself.

# Building the dataset

The other most common dataset used for Apriori analysis would be restricted to two columns. The first column will be the transaction ID and the second column will be the item related to the transaction ID. For example, let's consider that the transaction ID represents the users and the second column could be the items purchased by the user in case of a market basket analysis. In case of social media data, it could be the pages followed/liked by the users or in case of an e-commerce example, it could be the items purchased/viewed by the user. The data in the preceding format should be converted into a transactional data using the read.transactions function to read the data.

A simple dataset in the preceding format can be generated or derived in R. Such a simple dataset has been created, and you can find it with the following name. We will perform Apriori analysis on these two different datasets.

We can convert the data present in the CSV file into a transactional data using the `read.transactions` function. We can then briefly know about the data using the `summary` function as follows:

```
sampdata = read.transactions(file="following.csv", rm.duplicates= FALSE,
format="single",sep=",",cols =c(1,2));
summary(sampdata)
```

The output of the preceding code snippet is as follows:

```
> summary(sampdata)
transactions as itemMatrix in sparse format with
 79 rows (elements/itemsets/transactions) and
 501 columns (items) and a density of 0.4107229

most frequent items:
    i128     i187     i127     i134     i165 (Other)
      49       47       44       42       42   16032

element (itemset/transaction) length distribution:
sizes
   1    6    9   12   14   16   19   26   27   28   31   33   35   36   37   52   55   61   74
   1    1    1    1    1    2    1    1    1    2    1    2    1    1    1    1    1    1    1
  77   85   86   92   94   98   99  105  106  113  116  119  124  125  130  136  141  142  151
   1    1    1    1    1    1    1    1    1    1    1    1    1    1    1    1    1    1    1
 163  165  192  202  206  219  231  239  257  259  261  267  277  279  289  290  292  302  304
   1    1    1    1    1    1    1    1    1    1    1    1    1    1    1    1    1    1    1
 309  311  365  379  444  473  493  500
   1    1    1    1    1    1    1   12

    Min. 1st Qu.  Median    Mean 3rd Qu.    Max.
     1.0    58.0   142.0   205.8   303.0   500.0

includes extended item information - examples:
  labels
1     i1
2    i10
3   i100

includes extended transaction information - examples:
  transactionID
1             1
2            10
3            11
```

Thus, these are the two methods that will be sufficient to handle the transformation required for Apriori analysis in most of the dataset. The latter method is widely followed as, in most cases, the second column will be built based on a single item set rather than multiple sets.

# Apriori analysis

In order to perform Apriori analysis, we need to load the `arules` package. If the package has not been installed, use the `install.packages` function.

We can then apply the Apriori algorithm on the transactional data. In the previous section we created two different transactional datasets. Let's apply the Apriori algorithm on this dataset:

```
rules1<- apriori(Adult,parameter = list(sup = 0.5, conf =
0.9,target="rules"));
```

The output is as follows:

```
> rules1 <- apriori(Adult,parameter = list(sup = 0.5, conf = 0.9,target="rules"));

Parameter specification:
 confidence minval smax arem  aval originalSupport support minlen maxlen target    ext
        0.9    0.1    1 none FALSE            TRUE     0.5      1     10  rules FALSE

Algorithmic control:
 filter tree heap memopt load sort verbose
    0.1 TRUE TRUE  FALSE TRUE    2    TRUE

apriori - find association rules with the apriori algorithm
version 4.21 (2004.05.09)        (c) 1996-2004    Christian Borgelt
set item appearances ...[0 item(s)] done [0.00s].
set transactions ...[115 item(s), 48842 transaction(s)] done [0.05s].
sorting and recoding items ... [9 item(s)] done [0.01s].
creating transaction tree ... done [0.03s].
checking subsets of size 1 2 3 4 done [0.00s].
writing ... [52 rule(s)] done [0.00s].
creating S4 object  ... done [0.00s].
```

From the preceding output, we can see that there are 52 rules in total that are generated. In the preceding function, we use a few additional `sup` and `conf` parameters, which are nothing but `support` and `confidence`, respectively. We will explore these parameters in detail but, for now, we have the rules generated based on the inputs. We can then inspect the rules generated using the `inspect` function as follows:

```
inspect(rules1)
```

The following is the output:

```
> inspect(rules1);
  lhs                          rhs                      support confidence      lift
1 {}                        => {capital-gain=None}    0.9173867  0.9173867 1.0000000
2 {}                        => {capital-loss=None}    0.9532779  0.9532779 1.0000000
3 {hours-per-week=Full-time} => {capital-gain=None}    0.5435895  0.9290688 1.0127342
4 {hours-per-week=Full-time} => {capital-loss=None}    0.5606650  0.9582531 1.0052191
5 {sex=Male}                => {capital-gain=None}    0.6050735  0.9051455 0.9866565
```

The output is continued here:

```
22 {sex=Male,
    native-country=United-States} => {capital-gain=None}           0.5406003  0.9035349 0.9849008
23 {sex=Male,
    native-country=United-States} => {capital-loss=None}           0.5661316  0.9462068 0.9925823
24 {sex=Male,
    capital-gain=None}           => {capital-loss=None}            0.5696941  0.9415288 0.9876750
25 {workclass=Private,
    race=white}                  => {native-country=United-States} 0.5433848  0.9144157 1.0189334
26 {workclass=Private,
    race=white}                  => {capital-gain=None}            0.5472339  0.9208931 1.0038221
27 {workclass=Private,
    race=white}                  => {capital-loss=None}            0.5674829  0.9549683 1.0017732
28 {workclass=Private,
    native-country=United-States} => {capital-gain=None}           0.5689570  0.9218444 1.0048592
29 {workclass=Private,
    native-country=United-States} => {capital-loss=None}           0.5897179  0.9554818 1.0023119
30 {workclass=Private,
    capital-gain=None}           => {capital-loss=None}            0.6111748  0.9529145 0.9996188
```

 Note that this is just a random snapshot from the actual output.

This is how we generate the Apriori rules. From the preceding output, we got a frequent set of rules. Let's consider row number 28, for example. In this case, whenever `workclass` of a user is `Private` and `native-country` is `United-States` then it is most likely that `capital-loss` is `None`. The preceding code can be applied to the second transactional dataset and we can generate the rules. We also got the `support`, `confidence`, and `lift`. We will see one of them in detail.

# Support, confidence, and lift

The support, confidence, and lift are the important parameters to be set that define the output. Based on the business case, we set them accordingly. Let's see them in detail.

# Support

Support is an important measure in the process of extracting the association rules. It defines how often a rule is applicable in the dataset. For example, let's consider rule number 23 in the previous session, where we have {sex: "Male," native: "United States"}in lhs and {capital-loss: None} in rhs; here, it has support of "0.5661," which means that the number of transactions containing {sex: "Male", native: "United States", capital-loss: None} is about 56.61% of the total number of transactions.

Generally, the rules with very low support are neglected because they would have occurred mostly by chance, are not significant, and of no interest to the business as the chances of occurrence are very rare and not worth monitoring. However, in rare scenarios, when the number of transactions and item sets is enormous, there is a possibility that most of the occurrences might not be repeated and will result in very low support. For example, the number of people buying a pen and notebook would be smaller, compared to the other items bought, but this doesn't occur by chance.

# Confidence

Confidence is an equally important measure in the analysis of the association rules. It determines how frequently {capital-loss: None} occurs in the transactions that contain {sex: Mal, native: United States}. In our case, the confidence is 94.62%, which means that of all the transactions that have {sex: Male, native: United States}, 94.62% of the case, the value of capital loss was none. Thus, the confidence is a measure of consistency.

# Lift

Lift is the other most important parameter in filtering the rules. It indicates the degree to which the variable on the right-hand side, {capital-loss: None}, is most likely to be present whenever {sex: Male and native: United States} happens in the transactions.

{sex: "Male" and native: "United States" ☒ capital-loss: None}/ support{capital-loss: None}.

Hence, when the lift ratio is less than one, it means that the rule is less likely to occur and need not be focused. Thus, the rules are shortlisted based not only on the support and confidence, but also on the lift ratio, which should be greater than one. In our case, the lift ratio is less than one, so we can neglect the rule generated.

# Generating filtering rules

These rules are generated using the apriori function of the arules package. Let's generate the rules for the other dataset this time:

```
rules2<- apriori(sampdata,parameter = list(sup = 0.45, conf = 0.9,
target="rules"));
```

The following is the output of the preceding command:

```
> rules2 <- apriori(sampdata,parameter = list(sup = 0.45, conf = 0.9, target="rules"))

Parameter specification:
 confidence minval smax arem  aval originalSupport support minlen maxlen target   ext
        0.9    0.1    1 none FALSE          TRUE    0.45      1     10  rules FALSE

Algorithmic control:
 filter tree heap memopt load sort verbose
    0.1 TRUE TRUE  FALSE TRUE    2    TRUE

apriori - find association rules with the apriori algorithm
version 4.21 (2004.05.09)        (c) 1996-2004    Christian Borgelt
set item appearances ...[0 item(s)] done [0.00s].
set transactions ...[501 item(s), 79 transaction(s)] done [0.00s].
sorting and recoding items ... [105 item(s)] done [0.00s].
creating transaction tree ... done [0.00s].
checking subsets of size 1 2 3 done [0.00s].
writing ... [40 rule(s)] done [0.00s].
creating S4 object  ... done [0.00s].
```

We set the threshold for support as 0.45 and the threshold for confidence as 0.9. From the preceding output, we can see that there are about 40 rules generated. We can print them in descending order of their lift ratio using the following code:

```
inspect(head(sort(rules2, by="lift"),10))
```

The output is as follows:

```
> inspect(head(sort(rules2, by="lift"),10));
   lhs          rhs       support confidence      lift
1  {i128,
    i141} => {i139} 0.4556962  0.9473684 2.078947
2  {i141} => {i140} 0.4683544  0.9024390 1.926829
3  {i139} => {i141} 0.4556962  1.0000000 1.926829
4  {i140} => {i141} 0.4683544  1.0000000 1.926829
5  {i128,
    i139} => {i141} 0.4556962  1.0000000 1.926829
6  {i151} => {i146} 0.4556962  0.9729730 1.921622
7  {i146} => {i151} 0.4556962  0.9000000 1.921622
8  {i189} => {i200} 0.4556962  0.9000000 1.871053
9  {i200} => {i189} 0.4556962  0.9473684 1.871053
10 {i128,
    i134} => {i130} 0.4556962  0.9230769 1.869822
```

From the output, it is clear that whenever the i128 and i141 items co-occur, it is most likely that the i139 item will occur. Additionally, as the lift value is more than two, it further reiterates that the combination is most likely to occur. We can also get the top rules based on the combination of support, confidence, and lift using the quality function:

```
head(quality(rules2));
```

The output is as follows:

```
> head(quality(rules2));
    support confidence      lift
1 0.4556962  0.9473684 1.871053
2 0.4556962  0.9000000 1.871053
3 0.4556962  0.9729730 1.921622
4 0.4556962  0.9000000 1.921622
5 0.4556962  1.0000000 1.926829
6 0.4556962  1.0000000 1.612245
```

# Plotting

Let's plot and then see the sample dataset, sampdata. From the output, it is clear that the number of transactions is around 100 and number of items is around 500. The following code also includes saving the output to a local file in the current working directory:

# Dataset

```
image(sampdata)
dev.copy(png,filename="sampdata.png", width=600, height=875);
dev.off ();
```

The output of the preceding command is as follows:

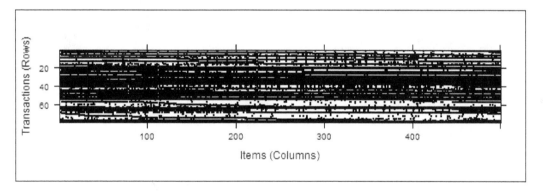

In the Adult dataset, the number of transactions is huge; if the number of items were fewer, it would appear as a straight line.

# Rules

In order to plot the rule, we need to load the `arulesviz` package to the R environment. If this package is not already installed, use the `install.packages` function to install it:

```
install.packages("arulesViz")
```
```
library(arulesViz)
```

We can plot the rules using the `plot` function. This plot will have the **support** and **confidence** in the $x$ axis and $y$ axis, respectively, and the shading is used to represent the lift. We can also change the representation using some of the parameters with the following code, where we have mentioned that the measure should be support and lift, that is, displayed through a scatter plot with the measure on the axes and confidence measured through shading:

```
plot(rules1)
```

The output of the preceding command is as follows:

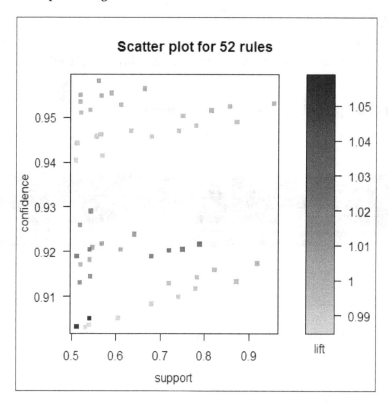

By default the rules are plotted with `support` and `confidence` on the x-axis and y-axis respectively, let's change it and see how it affects the plot:

```
plot(rules1, measure=c("support","lift"), shading="confidence")
```

The output is as follows:

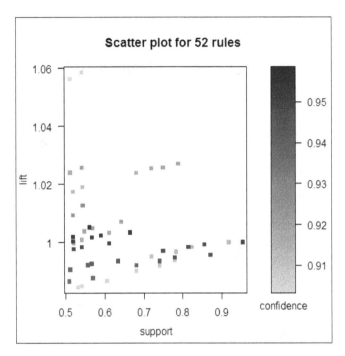

# Sequential dataset

So far, we generated various rules based on the transactions and events as well as the co-occurrence of various events. Now, we will consider the data along with the sequence in which the events happen. Sequence analysis is very popular to predict the occurrence of an event through a pattern from the historic data.

In order to understand sequence analysis, we will consider a sequential dataset. The `zaki` dataset contains sequential data that comes along with the `arulesSequences` package. We use the `summary` function to get the details of the sequential dataset. For better understanding, we convert the dataset into a data frame:

```
library(arulesSequences)
data(zaki)
summary(zaki)
```

The output of the preceding command is as follows:

```
> summary(zaki)
transactions as itemMatrix in sparse format with
  10 rows (elements/itemsets/transactions) and
  8 columns (items) and a density of 0.3375

most frequent items:
       A       B       F       C       D (Other)
       6       5       5       3       3       5

element (itemset/transaction) length distribution:
sizes
1 2 3 4
1 2 6 1

   Min. 1st Qu.  Median    Mean 3rd Qu.    Max.
   1.00    2.25    3.00    2.70    3.00    4.00

includes extended item information - examples:
  labels
1      A
2      B
3      C

includes extended transaction information - examples:
  sequenceID eventID SIZE
1          1      10    2
2          1      15    3
3          1      20    3
```

Let us have a look into the data using the following command:

**as(zaki, "data.frame")**

The output of the preceding command is as follows:

```
> as(zaki, "data.frame")
   transactionID.sequenceID transactionID.eventID transactionID.SIZE      items
1                         1                    10                  2      {C,D}
2                         1                    15                  3    {A,B,C}
3                         1                    20                  3    {A,B,F}
4                         1                    25                  4  {A,C,D,F}
5                         2                    15                  3    {A,B,F}
6                         2                    20                  1        {E}
7                         3                    10                  3    {A,B,F}
8                         4                    10                  3    {D,G,H}
9                         4                    20                  2      {B,F}
10                        4                    25                  3    {A,G,H}
```

This data frame conveys lots of information in a very friendly way for easy understanding. The `transactionID.size` parameter holds the number of items in the sequence and column items hold the actual items.

On the other hand, we can also create a data frame that holds the event sequence, and then we can convert it into a transactional dataset using the `read_baskets` function. However, it requires the data to hold three columns, namely, (`"sequenc eID"`,`"eventID"`,`"SIZE"`), where the combination of `sequenceID` and `eventID` is unique and `SIZE` holds the number of sequential events followed by the sequence of events separated by a comma.

As mentioned in the following code, the dataset named `sample` holds data as explained and is converted into a transactional data type so that it can be consumed by the Apriori sequence algorithm:

```
zaki <- read_baskets(con = "sample.txt", info = c("sequenceID","eventID",
"SIZE"))
```

# Apriori sequence analysis

Apriori sequence analysis is a technique that looks out for the statistically significant patterns in the sequence of the data. It is widely used in shopping use cases — we can predict what will be the likeliest next purchase on knowing the purchase of an item by a customer.

We can implement the Apriori sequence algorithm in R using the `cspade` function. In the following code, we filter the rules with `support` more than `0.55` alone:

```
seq_rules<- cspade(zaki, parameter = list(support = 0.55), control   =
list(verbose=TRUE))
```

The output is as follows:

```
> seq_rules <- cspade(zaki, parameter = list(support = 0.55), control   = list(verbose=TRUE)
)

parameter specification:
support : 0.55
maxsize :   10
maxlen  :   10

algorithmic control:
bfstype  : FALSE
verbose  :   TRUE
summary  : FALSE
tidLists : FALSE

preprocessing ... 1 partition(s), 0 MB [0.05s]
mining transactions ... 0 MB [0.01s]
reading sequences ... [0.05s]

total elapsed time: 0.11s
```

The preceding output will generate the rules based on the parameters specified. To learn about using other parameters, refer to the documentation of the packages at `https://cran.r-project.org/web/packages/arulesSequences/arulesSequences.pdf`.

# Understanding the results

We can check the details of the rules generated by the `cspade` function using the following code. The `summary` function provides you with a highlight about the dataset such as the number of sequences present in the dataset, the most occurring items, frequency table on the length of the sequence, and the distribution of the support measure:

```
summary(seq_rules)
```

The output of the preceding command is as follows:

```
> summary(seq_rules)
set of 18 sequences with

most frequent items:
      A       B       F       D  (Other)
     11      10      10       8      28

most frequent elements:
    {A}     {D}     {B}     {F}   {B,F} (Other)
      8       8       4       4       4       3

element (sequence) size distribution:
sizes
1 2 3
8 7 3

sequence length distribution:
lengths
1 2 3 4
4 8 5 1

summary of quality measures:
     support
 Min.    :0.5000
 1st Qu. :0.5000
 Median  :0.5000
 Mean    :0.6528
 3rd Qu. :0.7500
 Max.    :1.0000

includes transaction ID lists: FALSE

mining info:
 data ntransactions nsequences support
 zaki            10             4    0.55
```

We can take a look at the rules generated by converting them into a data frame using the following code. We can check the various sequences along with the support score for each of them. By default, the rules generated are sorted based on the support score.

```
as(seq_rules, "data.frame")
```

The output of the preceding command is as follows:

```
> as(seq_rules, "data.frame")
              sequence support
1               <{A}>   1.00
2               <{B}>   1.00
3               <{D}>   0.50
4               <{F}>   1.00
5             <{A,F}>   0.75
6             <{B,F}>   1.00
7         <{D},{F}>   0.50
8       <{D},{B,F}>   0.50
9           <{A,B,F}>   0.75
10            <{A,B}>   0.75
11        <{D},{B}>   0.50
12        <{B},{A}>   0.50
13        <{D},{A}>   0.50
14        <{F},{A}>   0.50
15    <{D},{F},{A}>   0.50
16      <{B,F},{A}>   0.50
17 <{D},{B,F},{A}>   0.50
18    <{D},{B},{A}>   0.50
```

# Reference

For details about the plotting of rules, refer to this wonderful blog at http://statistical-research.com/association-rule-learning-and-the-apriori-algorithm/.

For detailed documentation on the packages, refer to the following links:

- https://cran.r-project.org/web/packages/arulesSequences/arulesSequences.pdf

- https://cran.r-project.org/web/packages/arules/index.html

# Business cases

Having learnt about affinity analysis and sequence analysis, let's see the business cases across different domains where these techniques can be of use:

- In an online music playing website, we can understand about the sequence in which the users listen to the music where there is no automatic/shuffle

- In retail shops, we can understand the sequence in which the customer picks up the items and all the various items that the customer tends to buy together as well

- We can even understand about the career path of the individuals based on their career data from websites such as LinkedIn

# Summary

In this chapter, we understood the importance and usage of the transactional dataset, and Apriori rules, algorithms, and analysis that can be implemented on a transactional dataset with examples. The support, confidence, and lift parameters that define an output in an Apriori analysis have been covered. We have seen the filtering rules that can be generated and applied to a dataset. Moreover, we performed the plotting of a dataset in the form of graphs to provide a pictorial representation and understand the trends in a dataset more clearly. The sequential dataset that can be used to predict the occurrence of an event through a pattern from the historic data has been explained. Apriori sequence analysis techniques that look out for the statistically significant patterns in the sequence of the data have been explained. We have read and understood the dataset extracted and analyzed through the aforementioned analysis algorithms, and finally, an exercise to understand the sequence of music played in a playlist, grocery shopping sequence, and career path of an individual was given.

In the next chapter, we will demonstrate how and when to perform clustering analysis, how to identify the ideal number of clusters for a dataset, and how the clustering can be implemented using R. It also focuses on the hierarchical clustering — how it is different from normal clustering — and about the visualization of the clusters.

# 4
# Segmentation Using Clustering

Clustering is often considered a classic example of **unsupervised learning**. It is a method of dividing the dataset into multiple groups where the objects in the same group will be more similar to each other than those in the other groups.

Clustering algorithms are generally used on unlabeled datasets; hence, there is no way to measure the clustering output. The user, based on his requirement, should consider the variables carefully so that the resultant clusters closely match with the user's requirement.

The greatest example for the clustering algorithms would be a search engine where the pages that are closely related to each other are shown together and the pages that are different are kept apart as far as possible. The most important factor here is to measure the similarity or dissimilarity between the objects.

Some of the problems that can be solved through the implementation of clustering algorithms are the predicting of a disease in the medical field, matching the DNA to a suitable group, grouping the similar customers for the marketing campaigns, grouping the students based on their similarity in academics, and in various fields of research.

There are different methods of clustering based on the centroid, connectivity, distribution, and density. In this chapter, we will cover some of the clustering algorithms and their implementation using R. We will also cover some of the business use cases that can be solved using the clustering algorithms.

The topics that will be covered in this chapter are as follows:

- Datasets
- Centroid-based clustering and an ideal number of clusters
- Implementation using K-means
- Visualizing the clusters
- Connectivity-based clustering
- Visualizing the connectivity
- Other clustering algorithms and evaluation
- Business use cases

# Datasets

In this chapter, we will use a public dataset that was extracted from the website, `http://data.worldbank.org/`. We have pulled out the following details for all the countries. In case the data is not present for a country, it would appear blank.

We will use the following dataset to learn the concepts in this chapter. The extracted dataset is provided to you in a CSV file named `worlddata`. We will use the dataset to learn the concepts of clustering:

| Label | Description |
|---|---|
| electricity_access | The percentage of the population with electricity access |
| co2_emissions | Carbon dioxide emissions |
| mortality_rateper1000 | The mortality rate per thousand |
| export_percent_to_gdp | The exports in percentage to GDP |
| alternative_and_nuclearenergy_percent_total | Alternate and nuclear energy contribution from the whole dataset |
| forest_area_percent | Forests that are covered |
| net_migration | Net migration |
| male_unemployment | The unemployment rate in India |
| air_transport | Air traffic and registered carriers departure worldwide |
| brth_rate_per1000 | The birth rate per 1,000 |
| population_in1000s | The population |
| sanitation_access | The accessibility of sanitation |
| trade_in_services_percent_gdp | Services trading in percentage of GDP |
| expense_percent_gdp | The expense compared to the GDP |

| Label | Description |
|---|---|
| life_expectancy | The average life expectancy |
| gdp_in_millions | The GDP in millions |

# Reading and formatting the dataset in R

We can read the `worlddata` dataset from the local file using the `read` function. Check the following code before using the `read` function. We set the current working directory to the folder that holds the dataset using the `setwd()` function, and we can verify the working directory location using the `getwd()` function:

```
setwd("C:/book/Chapter 4")

getwd()

worlddata<- read.csv("data/worlddata.csv")
```

Now we have the dataset in the R environment in the data frame format. Before going into the formatting, let's understand about the dataset. We will use the `summary` function as well as print the top few rows to check the dataset:

```
summary(worlddata)
```

The output of the preceding command is as follows:

```
> summary(worlddata)
          country     electricity_access co2_emissions      mortality_rateper1000
 Afghanistan   :  1   Min.   :  5.00     Min.   :       51  Min.   :  2.00
 Albania       :  1   1st Qu.: 59.00     1st Qu.:     2245  1st Qu.:  8.00
 Algeria       :  1   Median : 96.00     Median :    18864  Median : 19.00
 American Samoa:  1   Mean   : 78.47     Mean   :   946092  Mean   : 35.11
 Andorra       :  1   3rd Qu.:100.00     3rd Qu.:   164592  3rd Qu.: 53.00
 Angola        :  1   Max.   :100.00     Max.   :34649483  Max.   :167.00
 (Other)       :243   NA's   :4          NA's   :17         NA's   :24
 export_percent_to_gdp alternative_and_nuclear.energy_percent_total
 Min.   :  6.00        Min.   : 0.000
 1st Qu.: 25.00        1st Qu.: 1.000
 Median : 35.00        Median : 4.000
 Mean   : 41.13        Mean   : 8.494
 3rd Qu.: 48.50        3rd Qu.:11.000
 Max.   :220.00        Max.   :90.000
 NA's   :90            NA's   :81
 forest_area_percent net_migration     male_unemployment air_transport
 Min.   : 0.00       Min.   :-17004655 Min.   : 0.000    Min.   :       0
 1st Qu.:11.00       1st Qu.: -120000  1st Qu.: 4.250    1st Qu.:   10856
 Median :31.00       Median :  -10000  Median : 7.000    Median :   42677
 Mean   :31.57       Mean   :  -71806  Mean   : 7.961    Mean   : 1125930
 3rd Qu.:45.00       3rd Qu.:   35000  3rd Qu.:10.000    3rd Qu.:  309502
 Max.   :95.00       Max.   : 16954933 Max.   :32.000    Max.   :31993334
 NA's   :11          NA's   :22        NA's   :43        NA's   :60
 brth_rate_per1000 population_in1000s sanitation_access trade_in_services_percent_gdp
 Min.   : 8.00     Min.   :       0   Min.   :  9.00    Min.   :  4.00
 1st Qu.:12.00     1st Qu.:    1314   1st Qu.: 49.50    1st Qu.: 12.00
 Median :19.00     Median :    8409   Median : 83.00    Median : 19.00
 Mean   :21.16     Mean   :  201060   Mean   : 72.42    Mean   : 26.03
 3rd Qu.:27.00     3rd Qu.:   38845   3rd Qu.: 98.00    3rd Qu.: 29.00
 Max.   :50.00     Max.   : 7207735   Max.   :100.00    Max.   :246.00
 NA's   :15                           NA's   :34        NA's   :72
 expense_percent_gdp life_expectancy gdp_in_millions
 Min.   : 0.00       Min.   :46.00   Min.   :     167
 1st Qu.: 20.00      1st Qu.:65.00   1st Qu.:   11964
 Median : 26.00      Median :73.00   Median :   57347
```

For `head(worlddata)`, the output is as follows:

```
> head(worlddata)
       country electricity_access co2_emissions mortality_rateper1000
1       Aruba                 91          2439                    NA
2     Andorra                100           491                     3
3 Afghanistan                 43         12251                    97
4      Angola                 37         29710                   167
5     Albania                100          4668                    15
6   Arab World                86       1704418                    40
  export_percent_to_gdp alternative_and_nuclear.energy_percent_total
1                    NA                                           NA
2                    NA                                           NA
3                     6                                           NA
4                    59                                            2
5                    36                                           20
6                    50                                            0
  forest_area_percent net_migration male_unemployment air_transport brth_rate_per1000
1                   2          1253                NA            NA                10
2                  34            NA                NA            NA                NA
3                   2       -399999                 7         25389                34
4                  47         65543                 7         13818                44
5                  28        -50002                18          1995                13
6                   2        354001                 9       1292823                26
  population_in1000s sanitation_access trade_in_services_percent_gdp
1                103                98                            NA
2                 80               100                            NA
3              31281                29                            25
4              22137                60                            19
5               2894                91                            36
6             377044                82                            15
  expense_percent_gdp life_expectancy gdp_in_millions
1                  NA              75              NA
2                  NA              NA              NA
3                  41              61           20842
4                  26              52          131401
5                  NA              78           13370
6                  NA              70         2855841
```

From the preceding two outputs, it is clear that the dataset we are using for our study has many missing values. We can't cluster the dataset with so many missing values, and so we need to handle the issue of the missing data. It can be handled by removing the missing values. We will use the `na.omit` function to remove all the rows that have blank values and it is preferred to have the attributes in a numerical format in order to perform clustering analysis. We can then check the new dataset using the `summary` function for the presence of any empty values in the rows and also for the distribution:

```
wdata<- na.omit(worlddata)
```
```
summary(wdata)
```

The output is as follows:

```
> summary(wdata)
        country      electricity_access co2_emissions        mortality_rateper1000
 Angola    : 1    Min.    : 15.00   Min.   :    1881   Min.    :   2.00
 Armenia   : 1    1st Qu.: 91.75   1st Qu.:   14113   1st Qu.:   4.00
 Australia : 1    Median :100.00   Median :   55652   Median :  11.00
 Austria   : 1    Mean    : 91.32   Mean   :  468793   Mean    :  20.87
 Azerbaijan: 1    3rd Qu.:100.00   3rd Qu.:  299085   3rd Qu.:  28.50
 Belarus   : 1    Max.    :100.00   Max.   : 6735121   Max.    : 167.00
 (Other)   :56
 export_percent_to_gdp alternative_and_nuclear.energy_percent_total
 Min.    : 12.00      Min.    : 0.00
 1st Qu.: 29.00      1st Qu.: 2.00
 Median : 40.00      Median : 5.50
 Mean    : 45.84      Mean    :11.53
 3rd Qu.: 54.00      3rd Qu.:18.75
 Max.    :188.00      Max.    :90.00

 forest_area_percent net_migration        male_unemployment air_transport
 Min.    : 0.00     Min.    :-13440900   Min.    : 0.000   Min.    :       0
 1st Qu.:15.50     1st Qu.:  -115762   1st Qu.: 5.000   1st Qu.:   17632
 Median :31.50     Median :        0   Median : 7.000   Median :   55590
 Mean    :29.65     Mean    :  -131451   Mean    : 8.613   Mean    :  527160
 3rd Qu.:38.75     3rd Qu.:   137501   3rd Qu.:10.750   3rd Qu.:  409706
 Max.    :73.00     Max.    :  5594633   Max.    :26.000   Max.    : 7463963
```

```
# Removing the column country
wdata<-  wdata[ , -which(names(wdata) %in% c("country"))]
```

The preceding code will remove the country column from the dataset that we will use to compute the clusters. Now, the dataset doesn't have any empty cells, but in order to perform clustering on the dataset, we have to convert it from the data frame format into a matrix format. Perform the following:

```
wdata<- data.matrix(wdata)
```

In the preceding dataset, we have multiple attributes with different ranges and so they are not really comparable with each other; thus, leaving us with no other option but to rescale the data so that equal weights are given and the computing distance for the clustering will make sense. The scale function will standardize the values to fall in similar ranges:

```
wdata<- scale(wdata)
```

# Centroid-based clustering and an ideal number of clusters

Centroid-based clustering is a method in which each cluster is represented by a central vector, and the objects are assigned to the clusters based on the proximity such that the squared distance from the central vector is minimized.

In this section, we will create the clusters using the **K-means** algorithm. We will see the implementation of this using R.

We need to use the `fpc` package called flexible procedure for the clustering in order to implement various clustering algorithms in R:

```
install.packages("fpc")
library(fpc)
```

Before creating the clusters using the K-means algorithm, we need to identify the ideal number of clusters for the given dataset. We can get the ideal number of clusters using the `pamk` function, where we do partitioning around the medoids to compute the ideal number of clusters. The `clusters$nc` variable will hold the ideal number of clusters:

```
clusters<- pamk(wdata)
n <- clusters$nc
n
[1] 5
```

The n vector will hold the value of the ideal number of clusters for the given dataset. This method of computing the ideal number of clusters is computationally intensive, so if the dataset is huge, then this method might be time-consuming. We will also cover an alternate method of manually computing the ideal number of clusters:

```
wss<- (nrow(wdata)-1)*sum(apply(wdata,2,var))

for (i in 2:25) wss[i] <- sum(kmeans(wdata,
centers=i)$withinss)
plot(1:25, wss, type="b", xlab="Number of Clusters",
ylab="Within groups sum of squares")


dev.copy(png,filename="elbowMethod.png", width=600, height=875);


dev.off ();
```

The preceding code is taken from Tal Galili's post based on *Chapter 16, R in Action, Second Edition, By Rob Kabacoff.* This will generate the plot mentioned here. We need to read the graph to get to know the ideal number of clusters for the dataset. As the number of clusters increases, the accuracy also tends to increase. For a dataset with n rows, if we have *n* clusters, then the sum of squared errors would be zero, but we need to stop at some ideal value practically. In the following graph, when the decrease in the sum of squared errors falls and is reduced to an extent that the increase in the number of clusters by one doesn't have an incremental value, then this is a point that represents the ideal number of clusters. It essentially means that a further increase in the number of clusters doesn't effectively decrease the error.

The elbow method chart is as follows:

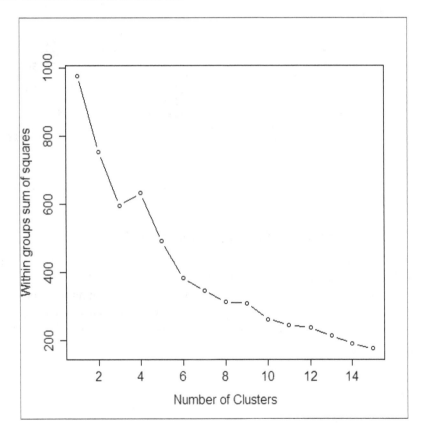

In most cases, the number of clusters by the partitioning around centroid-based clustering method as well as the elbow method would remain the same, but in this case, it is found to differ. We can still evaluate the ideal clusters using many more methods. The function that helps to compute the ideal number of clusters using multiple methods is `NbClust`; the following is an implementation of the same function on our dataset:

```
install.packages("NbClust")
library(NbClust)
NbClust(data = wdata, distance = "euclidean", min.nc = 2, max.nc = 20,
method = "average", index = "all", alphaBeale = 0.1)
```

The output is as follows:

|  | KL | CH | Hartigan | CCC | Scott | Marriot | TrCovW |
|---|---|---|---|---|---|---|---|
| Number_clusters | 5.0000 | 20.0000 | 5.0000 | 20.0000 | 13.0000 | 3.000000e+00 | 5.000 |
| Value_Index | 5.0851 | 15.6062 | 12.4186 | 9.1017 | 267.0163 | 1.197081e+20 | 3086.467 |

|  | TraceW | Friedman | Rubin | Cindex | DB | Silhouette | Duda | PseudoT2 |
|---|---|---|---|---|---|---|---|---|
| Number_clusters | 5.0000 | 13.000 | 8.0000 | 2.0000 | 2.0000 | | 2.0000 | 3.000 | 3.0000 |
| Value_Index | 111.5418 | 1418.375 | -0.3152 | 0.3249 | 0.3878 | | 0.5315 | 1.049 | -2.6164 |

|  | Beale | Ratkowsky | Ball | PtBiserial | Frey | McClain | Dunn | Hubert |
|---|---|---|---|---|---|---|---|---|
| Number_clusters | 3.0000 | 5.0000 | 3.0000 | 7.0000 | 2.0000 | 2.0000 | 7.0000 | 0 |
| Value_Index | -0.5072 | 0.2893 | 201.5503 | 0.7876 | 4.2294 | 0.0157 | 0.4425 | 0 |

|  | SDindex | Dindex | SDbw |
|---|---|---|---|
| Number_clusters | 11.000 | 0 | 15.0000 |
| Value_Index | 0.543 | 0 | 0.1034 |

# Implementation using K-means

After getting to know the ideal number of clusters, we can construct the required number of clusters in the dataset using the K-means method. We use the `kmeans` function to construct the clusters; this function takes the dataset as well as the number of clusters to be formed as an input. In the following case, we are just passing the number of clusters we want as an output from the `pamk` function:

```
fit<- kmeans(wdata, n)
table(fit$cluster)
1  2  3  4  5
3  3 27  7 22
```

As per the preceding output, there are five clusters with varying number of elements in each of the clusters. Even if an isolated element is not found similar to any of the existing clusters, it will be made to form a new cluster. We can see the mean of the elements in the clusters using the `aggregate` function. As we have to choose the mean to be the aggregation factor for all the attributes in the dataset, we get the mean for each of the clusters formed. If the clusters are mutually exclusive, then the aggregation results for the clusters will be different from one another:

```
# Cluster mean values
aggregate(wdata,by=list(fit$cluster),FUN=mean)
```

The output is as follows:

```
  Group.1 electricity_access co2_emissions mortality_rateper1000
1       1          0.4434092     3.2624870            -0.5076126
2       2         -0.6637402     2.0629932             1.2977569
3       3          0.2560455    -0.2196725            -0.1294609
4       4         -2.2867481    -0.3789316             1.9390465
5       5          0.4434092    -0.3360346            -0.5658325
  export_percent_to_gdp alternative_and_nuclear.energy_percent_total
1            -0.1875321                                    0.3738039
2            -0.7918455                                   -0.5377336
3            -0.3083948                                   -0.2490801
4            -0.3826390                                   -0.5637775
5             0.6337848                                    0.5074270
  forest_area_percent net_migration male_unemployment air_transport
1           0.4740945    2.07825747         0.4267416     3.9877966
2          -0.3959940   -3.32457438        -0.7650593     0.7032778
3          -0.2614876    0.07765924        -0.3148234    -0.1600973
4           0.2309021   -0.08766717        -0.5437248    -0.3928690
5           0.2367976    0.10253734         0.6055118    -0.3182051
  brth_rate_per1000 population_in1000s sanitation_access
1        -0.7206243          0.9533445         0.5951456
2         0.5898419          3.9347660        -1.9206970
3         0.1666705         -0.2340314         0.1558715
4         1.7950027         -0.2300375        -2.0019913
5        -0.7578534         -0.3061465         0.6264575
  trade_in_services_percent_gdp expense_percent_gdp life_expectancy gdp_in_millions
1                    -0.1270562           0.5576566     0.700631377       4.1318058
2                    -0.6051696          -0.9281597    -0.919277871       0.4915119
3                    -0.2864273          -0.3280681     0.009091172      -0.2001066
4                    -0.3059422          -0.6788391    -1.826670645      -0.3459615
5                     0.5487187           0.6691464     0.599871471      -0.2747884
```

Note that your output with the same dataset might be slightly different from the preceding output due to the randomness of the K-means algorithm.

# Visualizing the clusters

We can visualize the clusters created by the method using the `plotcluster` function. This function takes the original dataset as well as the elements of the clusters as an input. The output is different clusters with different colors for easy differentiation. The clusters are plotted based on the principal components of the features present in the dataset. The principal components are the combination of the features also called attributes present in the dataset:

```
# plotting the cluster
plotcluster(wdata, fit$cluster)
dev.copy(png,filename="scatterPlot.png", width=600, height=875);
dev.off ();
```

The output is as follows:

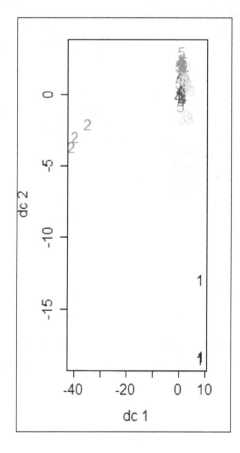

We can use the `clustplot` function to view the plot with better visualization; this function requires the packages `cluster` to be loaded to the R environment:

```
library(cluster)
```

```
clusplot(wdata, fit$cluster, color=TRUE, shade=TRUE, labels=1, lines=0)
```

The output is as follows:

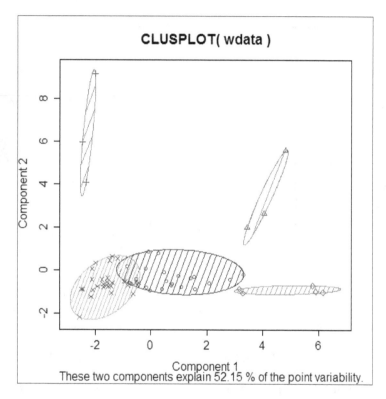

# Connectivity-based clustering

Connectivity-based clustering is also known as **hierarchical clustering**, where clustering analysis builds the cluster in an hierarchy. This method of clustering the dataset is considered not very suitable, especially when the dataset has too many outliers. Plotting the outliers in hierarchical clustering is complex and the computation process is time-consuming when the dataset is large.

In this section, we will oversee the implementation of hierarchical clustering using the same `worlddata` dataset in R. In order to implement hierarchical clustering, we first need to compute the distance for the elements in the dataset. We compute the distance between each and every element in the dataset using the `dist` function; this function takes the dataset as well as the method as an input, where we pass the methodology by which the distance is computed. This method can be used only for a numeric matrix. The different methods in which the distance is computed are `euclidean`, `maximum`, `manhattan`, `canberra`, `binary`, and `minkowski`:

```
distmeasure<- dist(wdata, method = "manhattan")
distmeasure
```

The output is as follows:

|    | 4 | 9 | 12 | 13 | 14 | 16 | 20 | 24 |
|----|---|---|----|----|----|----|----|----|
| 9  | 23.705064 | | | | | | | |
| 12 | 24.023906 | 8.877435 | | | | | | |
| 13 | 22.064184 | 9.789446 | 7.683454 | | | | | |
| 14 | 18.537129 | 6.918976 | 8.010754 | 9.858140 | | | | |
| 16 | 25.956323 | 9.546610 | 9.653731 | 5.772354 | 11.969788 | | | |
| 20 | 22.608060 | 5.524977 | 10.671671 | 6.017616 | 10.237577 | 6.754783 | | |
| 24 | 18.120688 | 8.200516 | 6.949959 | 5.208618 | 5.869587 | 8.629417 | 5.726772 | |
| 28 | 23.335939 | 10.882096 | 8.075510 | 9.901639 | 9.976264 | 14.475680 | 11.266241 | 8.768419 |
| 32 | 13.540282 | 14.629806 | 16.482793 | 18.725584 | 11.908294 | 19.241340 | 15.511352 | 13.906852 |
| 34 | 25.928802 | 8.903793 | 5.501254 | 7.995259 | 11.352792 | 9.456697 | 8.345774 | 8.656333 |
| 38 | 22.693620 | 7.219572 | 3.877113 | 6.643665 | 5.989764 | 8.553109 | 8.705384 | 5.835548 |
| 43 | 20.274446 | 9.052281 | 8.532642 | 9.182846 | 8.272011 | 12.912480 | 9.526087 | 7.305795 |
| 46 | 22.421001 | 7.141492 | 8.848494 | 6.259457 | 9.724219 | 9.727965 | 7.094106 | 6.565572 |

We use the `hclust` function to form hierarchical clustering, where we pass the distance computed in the previous methods as well as the method by which we are computing the hierarchies. In the following case, we use the `ward.D2` method.

Just print the clustering model to get to know about the rules generated by the `hclust` function. From the following image of the output, we get a basic understanding about the clustering such as the method used for the computation of the distance. The method through which we compute clusters also provides us with the number of objects in the dataset:

```
cluster<- hclust(distmeasure, method="ward.D2")
cluster
```

The output is as follows:

```
> cluster

Call:
hclust(d = distmeasure, method = "ward.D2")

Cluster method   : ward.D2
Distance         : manhattan
Number of objects: 62
```

# Visualizing the connectivity

We can visualize the hierarchical cluster generated using the `plot` function. To this function, we will pass the output of the `hclust` function and a few other graphical parameters related to the plotting. Let's see how the plot would look:

```
plot(cluster, cex=0.5, cex.lab=1, cex.axis=1, cex.main=1, cex.sub=1,
which.plots=2)
```

The output is as follows:

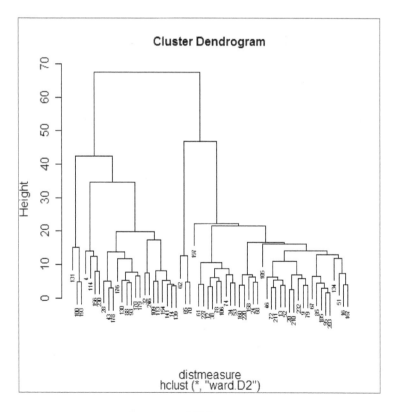

We can further divide the hierarchical cluster into different groups using the `rect.hclust` function. To this function, we pass the hierarchical `cluster` output, number of groups to be formed, and the `border` color to partition the output as parameters:

```
rect.hclust(cluster, k=5, border="red")
```

The output is as follows:

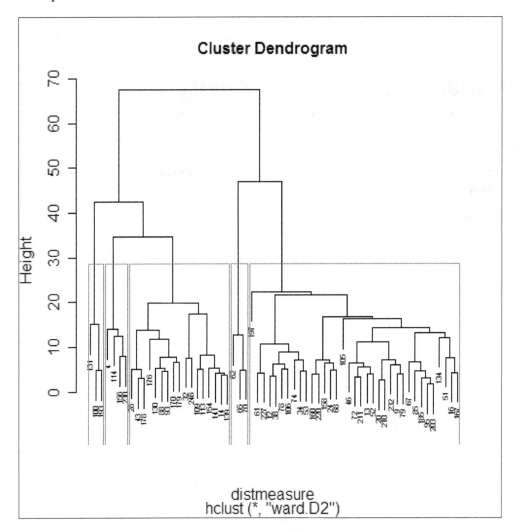

# Business use cases

The various use cases that can be solved with the help of clustering algorithms are as follows:

- A typical business case would be to launch a segmented marketing campaign, but in most cases, we would have the information to segment the customers with just a few attributes about the user. In order to divide the customers into different groups, we need to rely on the unsupervised algorithm. We can cluster the customers into different groups using an unsupervised centroid-based clustering method such as the K-means algorithm and can launch a segmented marketing campaign to these customer groups.

- Clustering algorithms are widely used in the field of research such as genetics clustering that helps in identifying a category that a particular species belongs to, grouping the medicines into different categories, identifying if the data shows up characteristics of any disease, and much more.

- Clustering algorithms also play an important role in the search engine field, where the search engine actually provides the results with the closest similarity.

- In academics, we can create a group of students based on various performance metrics so that every cluster would represent students of a different caliber and can be trained accordingly.

In general, we can use clustering algorithms in any cases where we have information on various characteristics about the dataset but don't have information on how the elements in the dataset are related to one another.

# Summary

In this chapter, we covered the prerequisites on the data format for the implementation of clustering algorithms and a few major clustering techniques, such as the centroid-based clustering algorithm, hierarchical clustering, and model-based and density-based clustering algorithms. We discussed about a few methodologies to evaluate the outcome of a clustering algorithm and various use cases across multiple fields that can be solved with the implementation of a clustering algorithm.

In the next chapter, we will demonstrate why regression models are used, the difference between a logistic regression and linear regression, and how to implement regression models using R. We will also explore the various methods used to check fit accuracy, the different methodologies that can be used to improve the accuracy of the model, and understand the output of regression models.

# 5
# Developing Regression Models

Regression analysis is a classic example of supervised learning. It's a method that helps you in knowing the relationship between a dependent variable and many other independent variables in the dataset.

The regression models can be broadly classified into logistic and linear models. In the case of logistic regression, the dependent variable is binomial and our output will be a probability of the categorical outcome; a problem of this nature is generally called a classification problem. On the other hand, in linear regression, the dependent variable is continuous in nature and the problems of this nature are called regression problems.

Let's take one example for each classification and regression problem. A typical classification model would be predicting if a banking customer would default his loan using various other details about the customer, such as his demographic, historic, and other details, whereas when we predict how much money a particular customer would default, then it is a regression problem.

In this chapter, you will learn to build logistic as well as linear regression models used to evaluate the predictions and improve the accuracy of the models.

The topics that will be covered in this chapter are as follows:

- Dataset
- Sampling the dataset
- Logistic regression
- Evaluating logistic regression

- Linear regression
- Evaluating linear regression
- Methods to improve the accuracy

# Datasets

In this chapter, we will use the `samepublic` dataset that was extracted from the website, `http://data.worldbank.org/`, in *Chapter 4, Segmentation Using Clustering*. In the case of the classification problem, we convert the `life_expectancy` column into a binomial variable by making the variable one if the life expectancy is more than 70; otherwise, the variable will be set to zero. The name of the dataset has been changed to `worlddata_ForClassification`. For the classification problem, we will consider the `life_expectancy_morethan_70` column as the column to be predicted and build the logistic regression algorithm:

```
# Data for Classification Problem
worlddatac<- read.csv("data/worlddata_ForClassification.csv")
```

After reading the preceding data, we will remove the rows that have NA values similar to what we did in the previous chapter, and we will remove the column named country as it is a unique column and will not help us in improving the accuracy of the model. After formatting the dataset, we will take a look at the dataset using the `head` function:

```
#Formatting the dataset
wcdata<- na.omit(worlddatac)
summary(wcdata)
names(wcdata)
wcdata<-  wcdata[ , -which(names(wcdata) %in% c("country"))]
head(wcdata)
```

The output is as follows:

| | electricity_access | co2_emissions | mortality_rateper1000 | export_percent_to_gdp |
|---|---|---|---|---|
| 4 | 37 | 29710 | 167 | 59 |
| 9 | 100 | 4961 | 16 | 31 |
| 12 | 100 | 369040 | 4 | 21 |
| 13 | 100 | 65203 | 4 | 54 |
| 14 | 100 | 33458 | 34 | 43 |
| 16 | 100 | 97766 | 4 | 84 |

| | alternative_and_nuclear.energy_percent_total | forest_area_percent | net_migration |
|---|---|---|---|
| 4 | 2 | 47 | 65543 |
| 9 | 27 | 9 | -50001 |
| 12 | 2 | 19 | 749997 |
| 13 | 13 | 47 | 150001 |
| 14 | 1 | 11 | 0 |
| 16 | 20 | 22 | 150007 |

| | male_unemployment | air_transport | brth_rate_per1000 | population_in1000s |
|---|---|---|---|---|
| 4 | 7 | 13818 | 44 | 22137 |
| 9 | 15 | 0 | 14 | 2984 |
| 12 | 6 | 644940 | 13 | 23491 |
| 13 | 5 | 162567 | 9 | 8534 |
| 14 | 4 | 18356 | 18 | 9538 |
| 16 | 9 | 134568 | 11 | 11225 |

| | sanitation_access | trade_in_services_percent_gdp | expense_percent_gdp |
|---|---|---|---|
| 4 | 60 | 19 | 26 |
| 9 | 91 | 22 | 23 |
| 12 | 100 | 8 | 26 |
| 13 | 100 | 27 | 38 |
| 14 | 82 | 17 | 22 |
| 16 | 100 | 42 | 45 |

| | gdp_in_millions | life_expectancy_morethan_70 |
|---|---|---|
| 4 | 131401 | 0 |
| 9 | 10882 | 1 |
| 12 | 1453770 | 1 |
| 13 | 436344 | 1 |
| 14 | 75198 | 1 |
| 16 | 533383 | 1 |

On the other hand, for the regression model, we will retain the dataset used in the previous chapter and consider the life_expectancy column as the dependent variable that has to be predicted. The formatting steps will remain the same in this case as well:

```
# Data for Regression
worlddata<- read.csv("data/worlddata.csv")
# formatting the dataset
wdata<- na.omit(worlddata)
wdata<-  wdata[ , -which(names(wdata) %in% c("country"))]
head(wdata)
```

The output is as follows:

```
    electricity_access co2_emissions mortality_rateper1000 export_percent_to_gdp
4                    37         29710                   167                     59
9                   100          4961                    16                     31
12                  100        369040                     4                     21
13                  100         65203                     4                     54
14                  100         33458                    34                     43
16                  100         97766                     4                     84
    alternative_and_nuclear.energy_percent_total forest_area_percent net_migration
4                                              2                  47         65543
9                                             27                   9        -50001
12                                             2                  19        749997
13                                            13                  47        150001
14                                             1                  11             0
16                                            20                  22        150007
    male_unemployment air_transport brth_rate_per1000 population_in1000s
4                   7         13818                44              22137
9                  15             0                14               2984
12                  6        644940                13              23491
13                  5        162567                 9               8534
14                  4         18356                18               9538
16                  9        134568                11              11225
    sanitation_access trade_in_services_percent_gdp expense_percent_gdp
4                  60                            19                  26
9                  91                            22                  23
12                100                             8                  26
13                100                            27                  38
14                 82                            17                  22
16                100                            42                  45
    life_expectancy gdp_in_millions
4                52          131401
9                75           10882
12               82         1453770
13               81          436344
14               71           75198
16               80          533383
```

# Sampling the dataset

While building the model, we need to have a training dataset that will be used to train the model, and then we will have a test dataset where the model that we built can be tested. Let's see the procedure to split the dataset into a training set and testing set:

```
# divide into sample
training_positions<- sample(nrow(wcdata), size=floor((nrow(wcdata)*0.7)))
```

The preceding code will take the sample of a specific size—in this case, it is 70% of the original dataset. We are considering 70% of the data as the training dataset and the remaining will be considered as the test dataset. The dataset will be randomly split; it is very important to split the dataset on a random basis in order to ensure consistency in the behavior mix of the data in the test set as well as the train set. We can use the `set.seed()` function to make sure that the output doesn't change while rerunning the code:

```
# Split into train and test based on the sample size
traindata<-wcdata[training_positions,]
testdata<-wcdata[-training_positions,]
```

Finally, using the following code, we get to know about the number of elements present in the training dataset as well as the test dataset:

```
nrow(traindata)
[1] 43
nrow(testdata)
[1] 19
```

# Logistic regression

In order to build a logistic regression in R, we generally use the `glm` function, which is nothing but a generalized linear model on the binary dependent variable. In the following section, you will learn to build the model to predict if the life expectancy for a country is more than 70 based on the other parameters, which we call the independent variables. These independent variables can either be continuous or categorical:

```
model<- glm(as.factor(life_expectancy_morethan_70)~., traindata,
family=binomial(link = "logit"))
```

In the preceding `glm` function, the first parameter that we pass is the dependent variable column that has to be predicted for the dataset. We will predict the `life_expectancy_morethan_70` column and the dot followed by the ~ symbol represents that we are considering all the others variables present in the dataset as independent variables. The next parameter that we mentioned is the name of the dataset and, in this case, the `traindata` data frame is the dataset. Finally, we set the `family` parameter as `binomial` and the link is specified as `logit`, which corresponds to the logistic regression. Note that while executing the preceding code, we might get a few warnings:

```
summary(model)
```

The output is as follows:

```
Call:
glm(formula = as.factor(life_expectancy_morethan_70) ~ ., family = binomial(link = "l
ogit"),
    data = traindata)

Deviance Residuals:
      Min          1Q      Median          3Q          Max
-7.744e-05   2.100e-08   2.100e-08   2.100e-08   5.728e-05

Coefficients:
                                               Estimate  Std. Error  z value  Pr(>|z|)
(Intercept)                                   -1.767e+03   7.569e+05   -0.002    0.998
electricity_access                             1.029e+01   4.096e+03    0.003    0.998
co2_emissions                                 -6.276e-05   1.412e-01    0.000    1.000
mortality_rateper1000                         -2.938e+00   1.381e+03   -0.002    0.998
export_percent_to_gdp                          1.124e+01   4.569e+03    0.002    0.998
alternative_and_nuclear.energy_percent_total   1.587e+00   5.598e+02    0.003    0.998
forest_area_percent                            1.483e+01   5.328e+03    0.003    0.998
net_migration                                  5.015e-05   2.490e-02    0.002    0.998
male_unemployment                              1.311e+01   5.906e+03    0.002    0.998
air_transport                                 -2.996e-04   1.500e-01   -0.002    0.998
brth_rate_per1000                              9.762e+00   4.463e+03    0.002    0.998
population_in1000s                             2.908e-04   1.875e-01    0.002    0.999
sanitation_access                              8.268e-01   1.671e+03    0.000    1.000
trade_in_services_percent_gdp                 -6.269e+00   2.745e+03   -0.002    0.998
expense_percent_gdp                            5.192e-01   1.874e+03    0.000    1.000
gdp_in_millions                                1.795e-04   1.777e-01    0.001    0.999

(Dispersion parameter for binomial family taken to be 1)

    Null deviance: 4.4121e+01  on 42  degrees of freedom
Residual deviance: 3.3964e-08  on 27  degrees of freedom
AIC: 32

Number of Fisher Scoring iterations: 25
```

We use the `summary` function to explore the model that has been built. The column estimate provides us with the intercept value as well as the coefficient for each of the independent variables in the dataset. Here, a positive value increases the probability of becoming one, whereas a negative value increases the probability of becoming zero. `Std. Error` is the standard error that is a measure for deviation from the estimate value. The `z` value explains the relationship between the dependent variable and each of the independent variables, whereas the `Pr` value is the significance value.

We have now built the model using the training dataset, and now we need to use the model to predict the values in the test dataset. In order to make the prediction, we can use the `predict` function. The various parameters that should be passed as the input to this function are `model` and the test dataset. We also pass the `type` parameter as `response` as we would need the output in terms of probability:

```
prediction<- predict(model, testdata, type="response")
```

All the predictions for the values in the test dataset are present in the vector prediction.

# Evaluating logistic regression

Now, after predicting the values in the test dataset, we need to compute the accuracy of the model to know where we stand. We will first combine the actual value and predicted values, and use the `head` function to visually see the difference between the actual and predicted values for a few of the rows. We will then convert the newly formed data into the data frame format. Based on a trial-and-error basis, we set a suitable threshold. In the following case, we consider the probabilities with a value greater than 0.7 as 1; otherwise, 0:

```
result<- cbind(testdata$life_expectancy_morethan_70, prediction)
result<- as.data.frame(result)
colnames(result) <- c("Actual","Prediction")
result$Predicted[result[2] > 0.7] <- 1
result$Predicted[result[2] <= 0.7] <- 0
result<-  result[ , -which(names(result) %in% c("Prediction"))]
head(result, 20)
```

The output is as follows:

| | Actual | Predicted |
|---|---|---|
| 13 | 1 | 1 |
| 14 | 1 | 0 |
| 16 | 1 | 1 |
| 28 | 1 | 1 |
| 34 | 1 | 0 |
| 38 | 1 | 1 |
| 52 | 1 | 1 |
| 61 | 1 | 0 |
| 62 | 1 | 1 |
| 74 | 1 | 1 |
| 154 | 0 | 0 |
| 170 | 0 | 0 |
| 176 | 0 | 0 |
| 178 | 1 | 1 |
| 193 | 0 | 0 |
| 197 | 1 | 1 |
| 203 | 1 | 1 |
| 220 | 1 | 1 |
| 227 | 1 | 0 |

From the preceding output, we can visualize the difference between the `Actual` and **Predicted** values. In order to get a quantitative measure, we use any of the following methods to get the score. The following function table will generate the confusion matrix:

```
xtab <- table(result$Predicted, result$Actual)
```

```
0  1

0   4  4

1   0 11
```

We can also use the `confusionMatrix` function to measure the accuracy, but as it is dependent on the `caret` package, we will install and load the package before executing it:

```
install.packages("caret")
```

```
library(caret)
```

```
confusionMatrix(xtab)
```

The output is as follows:

```
Confusion Matrix and Statistics


       0  1
0   4  4
1   0 11

                  Accuracy : 0.7895
                    95% CI : (0.5443, 0.9395)
       No Information Rate : 0.7895
       P-Value [Acc > NIR] : 0.6297

                     Kappa : 0.5366
    Mcnemar's Test P-Value : 0.1336

               Sensitivity : 1.0000
               Specificity : 0.7333
            Pos Pred Value : 0.5000
            Neg Pred Value : 1.0000
                Prevalence : 0.2105
            Detection Rate : 0.2105
      Detection Prevalence : 0.4211
         Balanced Accuracy : 0.8667

          'Positive' Class : 0
```

The output of the `confusionMatrix` function provides us with **Confusion Matrix** as well as some statistical data pertaining to the measure of **Accuracy** for the logistic regression. The detailed definition of the terms, **sensitivity** and **specificity**, can be found at the following URL:

```
https://en.wikipedia.org/wiki/Sensitivity_and_specificity
```

Thus, you learned about the implementation of the logistic regression and the steps involved in evaluating the performance of the outcomes. Now, we are good to proceed and implement a few more logistic regression use cases on our own.

# Linear regression

Building a linear regression model is very similar to building a logistic regression model. In simple linear regression, we predict the value of a dependent variable based on the value of other independent variables. In case of multiple linear regression, we will predict the dependent variable based on two or more independent variables.

Let's learn the implementation of linear regression using R. First, we need to divide the dataset into training and testing data. The code that is used to split the dataset is very similar to the code explained in the *Sampling the dataset* section. You can use the following code on the dataset that was created to explore the linear regression:

```
# divide into sample
training_positions<- sample(nrow(wdata), size=floor((nrow(wdata)*0.7)))
# Split into train and test based on the sample size
traindata<-wdata[training_positions,]
testdata<-wdata[-training_positions,]
nrow(traindata)
nrow(testdata)
```

The preceding code splits the dataset into a training set and testing set with a proportion of 70 and 30 respectively. We can change the proportion by tweaking the multiplication factor in the parameter size. Having split the dataset into two groups, let's build the model using the training dataset. The function to build the linear regression model is `lm`. We need to pass the column that has to be predicted followed by the ~ symbol and a dot representing the fact that we will consider all the other variables as independent variables that will be used to predict the dependent variable. Alternatively, we can also select the columns that should be used in order to predict the dependent variables. We also pass the name of the dataset as a parameter, and the dataset used in linear regression is named `traindata`:

```
model<- lm(life_expectancy~., traindata)
summary(model)
```

The output is as follows:

```
Call:
lm(formula = life_expectancy ~ ., data = traindata)

Residuals:
    Min      1Q  Median      3Q     Max
-14.8177 -1.7271  0.3197  1.9134  7.3115

Coefficients:
                                            Estimate Std. Error t value Pr(>|t|)
(Intercept)                                6.103e+01  1.154e+01   5.287 1.41e-05 ***
electricity_access                         6.473e-03  9.605e-02   0.067   0.9468
co2_emissions                             -1.094e-05  6.072e-06  -1.802   0.0827 .
mortality_rateper1000                     -1.183e-01  5.185e-02  -2.282   0.0306 *
export_percent_to_gdp                     -3.671e-02  4.943e-02  -0.743   0.4640
alternative_and_nuclear.energy_percent_total 3.411e-02 5.531e-02   0.617   0.5426
forest_area_percent                        3.748e-02  4.607e-02   0.814   0.4230
net_migration                             -2.289e-06  3.502e-06  -0.654   0.5190
male_unemployment                         -2.743e-01  1.826e-01  -1.502   0.1446
air_transport                              4.317e-06  7.175e-06   0.602   0.5524
brth_rate_per1000                         -5.177e-02  2.509e-01  -0.206   0.8381
population_in1000s                         1.152e-05  1.128e-05   1.021   0.3161
sanitation_access                          1.399e-01  9.911e-02   1.411   0.1696
trade_in_services_percent_gdp              1.231e-01  9.390e-02   1.311   0.2008
expense_percent_gdp                        9.327e-02  1.186e-01   0.786   0.4386
gdp_in_millions                            1.947e-06  2.128e-06   0.915   0.3683
---
Signif. codes:  0 '***' 0.001 '**' 0.01 '*' 0.05 '.' 0.1 ' ' 1

Residual standard error: 4.892 on 27 degrees of freedom
Multiple R-squared:  0.7536,    Adjusted R-squared:  0.6168
F-statistic: 5.506 on 15 and 27 DF,  p-value: 6.382e-05
```

The summary function has provided us with details about the linear regression model that has been built. The output would appear very similar to the one produced by the logistic regression. The estimate that appears in the preceding output is the coefficient for the independent variables. A positive value signifies that it has a positive relationship, whereas a negative value has a negative relationship. Std. Error is an estimate of the deviation of the coefficient. The t-statistic value is the coefficient, that is, the estimate divided by the standard error. The final column tells us the significance of the variables. From the preceding output, we can understand that the mortality_rateper100 variable has a significance less than 0.05 and the cO2_emissions variable has a significance score of about 0.08, which falls under 10%. This means that these two variables have a higher impact in predicting the life expectancy accurately.

Having built the model, you will learn to use it to make a prediction. The predict function can be used to make the prediction. In case of linear regression, we will pass model as well as the test dataset as the input parameters. The vector prediction will hold all the prediction values for the test dataset:

```
prediction<- predict(model, testdata)
```

In order to compare the predicted value with the actual value, we need to combine the values. This can be performed using the cbind function. Then, we use the as.data.frame function to convert it into a data frame:

```
result<- cbind(testdata$life_expectancy, prediction)
result<- as.data.frame(result)
colnames(result) <- c("Actual","Prediction")
head(result, 50)
```

The output is as follows:

```
      Actual  Prediction
9         75    72.75981
13        81    81.03495
16        80    80.27741
34        81    77.75966
46        80    78.45215
51        80    80.94658
65        81    91.58742
70        80    93.95898
74        82    83.63766
93        74    73.18376
95        77    76.28783
109       74    73.25819
131       67   103.22019
134       74    82.12733
156       50    57.95846
170       68    64.81323
179       69    72.65387
193       67    80.55907
203       75    74.49725
```

# Evaluating linear regression

The evaluation of linear regression is different from what we did in logistic regression. The most common method of evaluating a linear regression problem is based on the mean squared error rate. This can be implemented using the following code:

```
#evaluation for the regression - mean squared error
sqerr<- (result$Actual-result$Prediction)^2
meansqerr<- sum(sqerr)/nrow(result)
meansqerr
[1] 104.1653
```

The preceding value is the error rate. We can tune the linear regression model until we arrive at the lowest error score.

# Methods to improve the accuracy

We will explore some of the different methods that can be performed to improve the accuracy of the model. Note that these are just techniques that can be tried; they can't guarantee improvement in the accuracy. Some of the methods might work for some kinds of data. Let's understand the popular options available to us.

# Ensemble models

We will build multiple algorithms and combine the results of different algorithms with different weightages. We can decide on the weightage based on a trial-and-error basis. As discussed previously, the dataset can be divided into a training set and testing set, and we can evaluate the performance with different weightages.

The other popular regression models that can be implemented are **Support Vector Machine** (**SVM**) and **Random Forest**. The SVM algorithm is where the model is built by constructing a hyperplane, and in random forest, we build the model by building a number of decision trees.

# Replacing NA with mean or median

When there are very few records with blank or NA values, then we can also consider replacing them with the average value. This methodology may or may not help in improving the accuracy, and so, it is important to test the performance on a sample test data. This can be implemented using the following code.

It is preferred to replace the missing values with the median rather than the mean value because the presence of a few outliers could skew the mean value, whereas it will not affect the median value:

```
# Actual data
worldd<- read.csv("data/worlddata.csv")
worldd<-  worldd[ , -which(names(worldd) %in% c("country"))]
worldd<- as.matrix(worldd)
head(worldd)
```

The output is as follows:

| | trade_in_services_percent_gdp | expense_percent_gdp | life_expectancy | gdp_in_millions |
|---|---|---|---|---|
| [1,] | NA | NA | 75 | NA |
| [2,] | NA | NA | NA | NA |
| [3,] | 25 | 41 | 61 | 20842 |
| [4,] | 19 | 26 | 52 | 131401 |
| [5,] | 36 | NA | 78 | 13370 |
| [6,] | 15 | NA | 70 | 2855841 |

 Note that the preceding screenshot is just a part of the output.

Let us write code to replace the NA values with the median value:

```
# Replacing with the Median value
worldd[is.na(worldd)] <- median(worldd, na.rm=TRUE)
head(worldd)
```

The output is as follows:

| | trade_in_services_percent_gdp | expense_percent_gdp | life_expectancy | gdp_in_millions |
|---|---|---|---|---|
| [1,] | 52 | 52 | 75 | 52 |
| [2,] | 52 | 52 | 52 | 52 |
| [3,] | 25 | 41 | 61 | 20842 |
| [4,] | 19 | 26 | 52 | 131401 |
| [5,] | 36 | 52 | 78 | 13370 |
| [6,] | 15 | 52 | 70 | 2855841 |

 Note that the preceding screenshot is just a part of the output.

Let us write code to replace the NA values with the mean value:

```
# Replacing with the mean value
worldd[is.na(worldd)] <- mean(worldd, na.rm=TRUE)
head(worldd)
```

The output is as follows:

| | trade_in_services_percent_gdp | expense_percent_gdp | life_expectancy | gdp_in_millions |
|---|---|---|---|---|
| [1,] | 296929.4 | 296929.4 | 75.0 | 296929.4 |
| [2,] | 296929.4 | 296929.4 | 296929.4 | 296929.4 |
| [3,] | 25.0 | 41.0 | 61.0 | 20842.0 |
| [4,] | 19.0 | 26.0 | 52.0 | 131401.0 |
| [5,] | 36.0 | 296929.4 | 78.0 | 13370.0 |
| [6,] | 15.0 | 296929.4 | 70.0 | 2855841.0 |

Note that the preceding screenshot is just a part of the output.

# Removing the highly correlated values

This method is more apt when the number of independent variables is large. When we build a model with a large number of independent variables, there is a possibility for an increased error rate as the errors also amplify with increasing variables. Hence, we should remove the duplicate columns — this can be achieved by computing the correlation between the variables — and then, we can remove the variables that have a high correlation.

This can be implemented as shown in the following code; read the comments (statements followed by #) to understand the code better:

```
# Initial number of columns
ncol(worldd)
[1] 16
library(caret)
# Identify the column pairs with correlation more than 0.9
tooHigh<- findCorrelation(cor(worldd[,1:16]), .9)
# The column number 9 is duplicated
tooHigh
[1] 9
# remove those highly correlated columns
worldd<-worldd[,-tooHigh]
# Total number of columns after removal
ncol(worldd)
[1] 16
```

# Removing outliers

The presence of outliers may or may not help in improving the accuracy of the model. Generally, when the occurrences of outliers are few in the dataset, it is recommended that you remove them while building the model as they might skew the results. When the number of outliers is large, it essentially conveys the dynamic nature of the data, so in these cases, it would be advisable to retain the outliers in the dataset.

The outliers in the data can be removed using the following code. The `outlier` function needs the `outliers` package to be loaded. Read the comments to understand the code better. In the following case, a large number of values have been considered outliers; hence, it looks like having an outlier is a normal behavior of the dataset. In such a case, it is advisable not to perform the outlier removal process but to retain them in predicting the dependent variable:

```
# Package required for using the function outlier
library(outliers)
#Identifying the outliers in the dataset
outlier_tf = outlier(worldd,logical=TRUE)
#Number of outliers in the dataset
sum(outlier_tf)
[1] 518
#Positions of the outliers
find_outlier = which(outlier_tf==TRUE,arr.ind=TRUE)
#Removing the outliers
worldd = worldd[-find_outlier,]
# Number of rows after removing the outliers in the dataset
nrow(worldd)
[1] 62
```

These techniques might help in improving the accuracy of both the logistic as well as the linear regression models. Generally, one or more of these could work well for a particular dataset. Instead of building the model and testing the test data, it is preferred to split the training data, build the model, and test the performance before going to the final prediction.

# Summary

We acquired the capability to build the logistic as well as linear regression models. You also learned to evaluate the model internally on the given dataset by randomly splitting them into two different datasets, read the output of the models, make business interpretations, and some really important techniques that can be used to improve the accuracy of the model. Most importantly, you learned the scenarios in which these algorithms can be of use to us.

In the next chapter, we will cover the forecasting based on the time series data, which can be really helpful in predicting sales, and help us plan accordingly.

# 6

# Time Series Forecasting

Forecasting is the process of predicting future events based on historic data. When forecasting is made on a time series data, such as events happening over a time interval, then it is called time series forecasting.

The time series forecasting can be implemented in multiple ways; it can be a simple moving average of the historic values or it can be built considering the factors such as the seasonality component and trend component. The seasonality component is one that has a cyclic behavior and repeats over a fixed time interval, whereas a trend component is generally short-lived and a gradual change that can move the value either upward or downward.

Time series forecasting has been in use across multiple industries for quite some time; it is commonly used for sales forecasting so that the raw material can be procured accordingly. The famous example for forecasting is weather forecasting, where based on the pattern in the past and recent changes, the future can be predicted. These predictions are very important to plan the power generations/procurements to avoid unnecessary power disruptions or overproduction as last minute procurements are expensive and wastage is inexcusable. Additionally, in the case of supply chain management, there is always a requirement for demand forecast, and in the case of retailers, there is a need for sales forecast.

In this chapter, you will learn how to extract the seasonality and trend components from the data as well as make predictions using **autoregressive integrated moving average** (**ARIMA**), which is a moving average method, and the **Holt-Winters** method.

The topics that will be covered in this chapter are as follows:

- Using the time series dataset
- Extracting patterns
- Forecasting using ARIMA
- Forecasting using Holt-Winters
- Discussing the methods to improve accuracy

# Datasets

In this chapter, we will use the temperature dataset of Massachusetts; this public dataset was downloaded from `http://cdiac.ornl.gov/`. This dataset holds the maximum temperature recorded at Massachusetts on a daily basis from 1980 to 2010. The temperature in this dataset is rounded off to an integer and the missing values are represented as NA. We will use this dataset to learn about the techniques involved in the forecasting algorithm.

 Note that changes in terms of representation of the data have been made to make the dataset more R-friendly in terms of reading and computing.

Let's have a look at the dataset by reading the dataset to the R environment:

```
# reading the dataset
data <- read.csv("Data/msdata.csv")
head(data, 10)
```

The output of the preceding code is as follows:

|     | date      | maxTemp |
|-----|-----------|---------|
| 1   | 1/1/1980  | 40      |
| 2   | 1/2/1980  | 43      |
| 3   | 1/3/1980  | 38      |
| 4   | 1/4/1980  | 32      |
| 5   | 1/5/1980  | 34      |
| 6   | 1/6/1980  | NA      |
| 7   | 1/7/1980  | 27      |
| 8   | 1/8/1980  | 46      |
| 9   | 1/9/1980  | 40      |
| 10  | 1/10/1980 | 32      |

The preceding dataset needs some modifications, such as the date format has to be changed to one that will be supported for the time series analysis and the missing values in the dataset have to be replaced with the appropriate values. We will show how to implement these changes to the dataset.

First, we can change the format of the data using the following code:

```
data$date <- as.Date(data$date, "%m/%d/%Y")
```

To know more about the date and time format, check using the strptime command. Now, we need to replace the NA values with the most appropriate values. The best method to implement this would be to compute the average on the date basis as we have a good set of historic data, and whenever the values are found missing, we can replace them with the average value for the particular missing day based on the historic values of the same day's data. This can be implemented using the following code:

```
# create day - month column
data$dayMonth <- strftime(data$date, format="%m-%d")
# compute the average for the day - month combination
data <- transform(data, mavg =ave(maxTemp,dayMonth, FUN=function(x)
mean(x,na.rm=TRUE) ))
# replace the missing value with the mean
newdata <- transform(data, maxTemp =ifelse(is.na(maxTemp),mavg,maxTemp))
head(newdata)
```

The output of the preceding code is as follows:

```
        date maxTemp dayMonth      mavg
1 1980-01-01    40.0    01-01 40.90323
2 1980-01-02    43.0    01-02 40.87097
3 1980-01-03    38.0    01-03 41.54839
4 1980-01-04    32.0    01-04 40.64516
5 1980-01-05    34.0    01-05 39.90000
6 1980-01-06    39.4    01-06 39.40000
```

```
# selecting required data
tsdata <- data.frame(newdata$date,newdata$maxTemp)
colnames(tsdata) <- c("date","maxTemp")
head(tsdata, 10)
```

The output of the preceding code is as follows:

```
      date maxTemp
1  1980-01-01    40.0
2  1980-01-02    43.0
3  1980-01-03    38.0
4  1980-01-04    32.0
5  1980-01-05    34.0
6  1980-01-06    39.4
7  1980-01-07    27.0
8  1980-01-08    46.0
9  1980-01-09    40.0
10 1980-01-10    32.0
```

We replaced the missing values with the corresponding mean value. However, as the dataset doesn't capture any data for the date, February 29, we need to remove it from the dataset. This can be implemented using the following code:

```
# Remove NaN values - dont use
tsdata <- tsdata[complete.cases(tsdata), ]
```

We can also check whether there are any NA values by computing `mean` for the `maxTemp` column. If we get a numeric value as the output, we are good to move forward:

```
mean(tsdata$maxTemp)
[1] 60.65281
```

We formatted the data as required and we will now convert the data into a time series dataset so that we can build the forecasting models:

```
# converting to timeseries
ts=ts(tsdata$maxTemp, start=c(1980,1),frequency=365)
head(ts)
[1] 40.0 43.0 38.0 32.0 34.0 39.4
```

Let's plot the time series data using the `plot` function:

```
plot(ts)
```

The output of the preceding command is as follows:

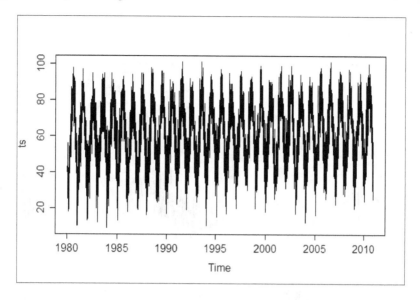

The preceding plot shows us the time series data. We have the data from **1980** till **2010**. We will use the preceding time series data for all the forecasting.

# Extracting patterns

From the plot of the time series data mentioned in the preceding session, we can clearly see the seasonality patterns. Now we will see the ways to extract the seasonality component and trend component. This can be implemented using the `stl` function also called **Seasonal Decomposition of Time** series by Loess. This method decomposes the dataset into seasonal, trend, and irregular components using the Loess method. Loess is a method of estimating nonlinear relationships.

First, we will consider a subset of data from the time series dataset for a better visualization of the components. We can extract a subset of data using the `window` function, which takes the time series data itself as an input along with the `start` and `end` dates. In the `start=c(2007,1)` parameter, 2007 is the start year and 1 is the start month in the year 2007. Hence, the following code creates a subset ranging from 2007 to 2009. After subsetting the dataset, we will use the `plot` function to visualize the output:

```
newWindow = window(ts, start=c(2007,1), end=c(2009,12 ))
plot(newWindow)
```

The output of the preceding command is as follows:

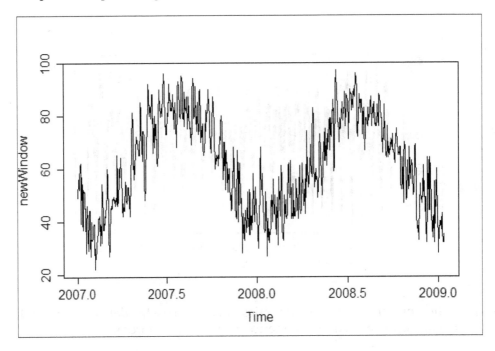

Now, from the preceding subset, we extract the seasonality and trends using the `stl` function. We need to pass the time series data as a parameter to the `stl` function, and using the `s.window` parameter, we can extract the seasonality component. By default, we can set the `s.window` parameter as periodic; alternatively, we can specify the span of the Loess window:

```
decompose1 = stl(newWindow, s.window="periodic")
plot(decompose1)
```

The output of the preceding code is as follows:

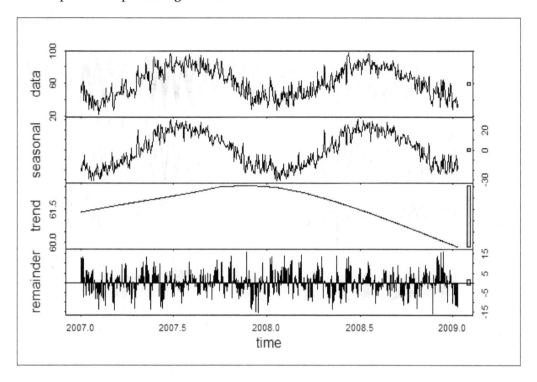

In the preceding output, we can see that the **seasonal**, **trend**, and **remainder** components have split. While defining the `stl` function, we had only specified about the seasonality component, whereas the default is considered for the other components.

We will now make use of a few more parameters and see how the output changes. Using the following code, we define the `t.window` parameter through which we define the span of the Loess windows to extract the trend component. In the following code, we define the span for the trend window as `60`. We also set the `robust` parameter as `TRUE`, which means that `robust` fitting will be used for the Loess procedure:

```
decompose2 = stl(ts, s.window="periodic", t.window=60, robust=TRUE)
plot(decompose2)
```

The output of the preceding command is as follows:

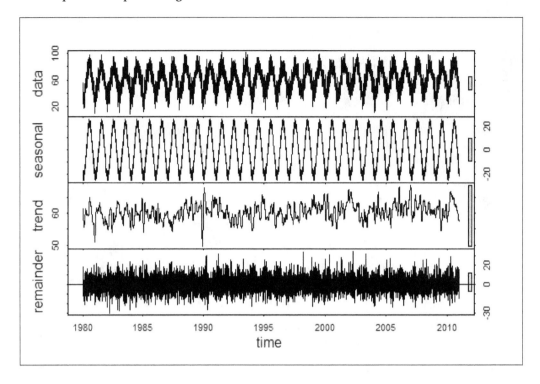

By tweaking the parameters, we can clearly see that the components have changed. Thus, we have covered the important concepts in the extraction of patterns. In order to know more about the parameters of the `stl` function, refer to the following links:

- `https://stat.ethz.ch/R-manual/R-devel/library/stats/html/stl.html`

- `https://cran.r-project.org/web/views/TimeSeries.html`

- `https://www.otexts.org/fpp/6/5`

Thus, you learned the procedures involved in extracting the patterns. We will now proceed to the forecasting techniques. To build the forecasting model, we need to install the `forecast` package and load it to the R environment:

```
install.packages("forecast")
```

```
require("forecast")
```

# Forecasting using ARIMA

We can build the ARIMA forecasting model using the `arima` function in R. The following code is used to build the ARIMA forecasting model, which can be used to make the forecast:

```
a_model=arima(as.matrix(ts), order=c(2,0,0))
```

There are a few important concepts that we should know in the implementation of the ARIMA technique. The preceding function takes the time series data as an input, and the other mandatory parameter that has to be passed is the order parameter, which requires three values (p, d, q), defined as follows:

- p: The number of autoregressive terms
- d: The number of nonseasonal differences needed for stationarity
- r: The number of lagged forecast errors

We will understand how to choose the preceding values to build the forecasting model. We will go through a few of the combinations in detail, as shown here:

- (1,0,0): This series is generally used when the data is highly auto-correlated. Here, we predict the current value using its immediate preceding value. Usually, the current value will be predicted by multiplying the previous value with a multiplicative factor plus a constant.
- (2,0,0): In this case, the current value is predicted based on the preceding two values.
- (0,1,0): This is also called a random walk model, where there is neither seasonality nor can the previous value predict the current value.
- (1,1,0): This case is used when the random walk model has a drift that can be defined by the previous value.
- (0,1,1): This method can be used when there is no seasonality or trend in the data. This is also called the simple exponential smoothening method. In this case, the error of the random walk is offset by the smoothening of the previous value.

These are a few of the combinations; in order to understand each of the combinations in detail, refer to the following links:

- http://people.duke.edu/~rnau/411arim.htm
- https://www.otexts.org/fpp/7/1
- http://people.duke.edu/~rnau/411arim2.htm
- http://people.duke.edu/~rnau/411arim3.htm

Now that we have built the ARIMA model, we will use it to forecast the future data. We will use the `forecast.Arima` function in order to forecast the future values. We pass the model itself as a parameter to the `forecast` function, and then we also need to pass the number of future values that has to be predicted. In the following case, we are predicting the future 10 years of value based on three decades of data:

```
aforecast=forecast.Arima(a_model,h=3650)
```

```
plot(aforecast)
```

The output of the preceding command is as follows:

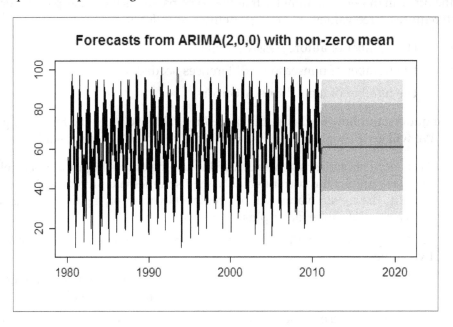

You can now tweak the `order` parameter that is used to build the model and see the effect on the prediction. Let's see how the simple exponential smoothening model will look:

```
a_model=arima(as.matrix(ts), order=c(0,1,1))
```

```
aforecast=forecast.Arima(a_model,h=3650)
```

```
plot(aforecast)
```

The output of the preceding command is as follows:

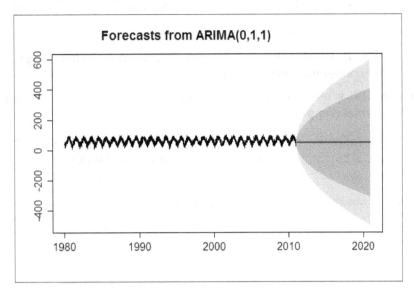

In this case, we can clearly see that the error could be really high as the range is now between -500 to 500, whereas previously, it was in the range of 20 to 90. We can use the following code to print the output in the required directory:

```
dev.copy(png,filename="arimaf2.png", width=600, height=400);
dev.off ();
```

Thus, you learned about forecasting using the ARIMA model. In this case, it had been difficult to control the seasonality factor based on limited parameters. We will see how to improve the accuracy using some advanced forecasting algorithms that better capture the trend and seasonality.

# Forecasting using Holt-Winters

We will now explore the methods of building the forecasting model using the Holt-Winters method with the `HoltWinters` function, which belongs to the `forecasting` package. This function computes the Holt-Winters filtering for a given time series data, and the unknown parameters are determined by minimizing the squared prediction error.

Apart from passing the time series data as an input, the other important parameters that need to be passed to this function are the alpha, beta, and gamma, as follows:

- `alpha`: The parameter of the Holt-Winters filters
- `beta`: This is used for the trend component; when set to false, the function will do exponential smoothening
- `gamma`: This is used for the seasonal component; when set to false, the nonseasonal component is fitted

Let's execute the following code where the trend component is set to FALSE, and hence, exponential smoothening will be performed on the dataset. We have set the gamma value as 0.5:

```
h_model=HoltWinters(ts, beta=FALSE, gamma=0.5)
plot(h_model)
```

The output of the preceding command is as follows:

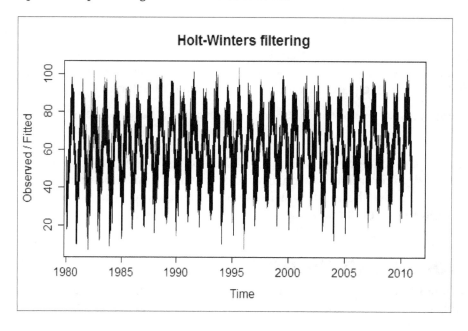

Based on the preceding model, we will forecast the future using the `predict` function. We need to pass the model that was built using the Holt-Winters technique to the `predict` function. The other parameters that have to be passed are the period (for which the prediction has to be made), `prediction.interval` (when set to true, the lower and upper bounds of the corresponding prediction intervals are computed), and level (which is the confidence interval for the prediction):

```
# plot forecasting with confidence interval
forecast <- predict(h_model, n.ahead = 3650, prediction.interval = T,
level = 0.1)
plot(h_model, forecast)
```

The output of the preceding command is as follows:

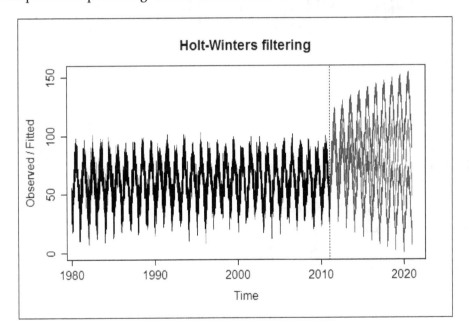

We will change the `gamma` value and see how it affects the forecasting. From the following output, we can clearly see that reducing the `gamma` value has also reduced the prediction range; now it is more in line with the historic data:

```
h_model=HoltWinters(ts, beta=FALSE, gamma=0.1)
forecast <- predict(h_model, n.ahead = 3650, prediction.interval = T,
level = 0.1)
plot(h_model, forecast)
```

The output of the preceding command is as follows:

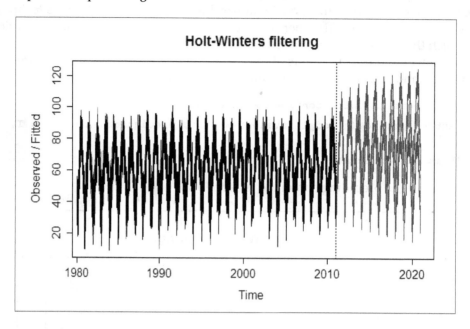

In order to see the actual forecasted value, we will use the following code. The vector that holds the forecasted value can be used. In the following code, we format the data in such a way that we get the predicted value as a data frame:

```
hforecast <- as.data.frame(forecast)
predscore <- hforecast$fit
predscore <- as.data.frame(predscore)
head(predscore, 10)
```

The output of the preceding command is as follows:

|    | x        |
|----|----------|
| 1  | 42.15262 |
| 2  | 42.47563 |
| 3  | 44.20206 |
| 4  | 42.34926 |
| 5  | 40.16073 |
| 6  | 38.78335 |
| 7  | 39.64009 |
| 8  | 39.22190 |
| 9  | 38.45621 |
| 10 | 35.35218 |

To know more about the Holt-Winters algorithm and parameters, refer to the following link:

```
https://stat.ethz.ch/R-manual/R-patched/library/stats/html/
HoltWinters.html
```

# Methods to improve accuracy

There are a few general methods that help in improving the accuracy of the forecasting model. In this section, we will have a brief discussion about these methods.

The widely used method is to split the dataset into training and testing. Build the forecasting model using the training dataset and test for the accuracy using the testing dataset. Rebuild the forecasting model by tweaking the parameters until the error is minimal.

The other method is to combine multiple algorithms and compute the weighted average in order to arrive at the final prediction.

As the seasonality and trend have a high influence on the forecasting model, it is better to keep updating the forecasting model on a frequent basis.

# Summary

In this chapter, you learned how to convert a dataset into a time series dataset and how to extract the seasonal and trend components from the data. We acquired the capability to build a forecasting model using the ARIMA and Holt-Winters models and also got a brief introduction to the details of the parameters involved in the models to help in tweaking for better accuracy. Finally, we completed the chapter with methods to help in improving the overall accuracy.

In the next chapter, we will cover the concepts and implementation of recommendation systems using the collaborative filtering algorithm.

# 7
# Recommendation Engine

A recommendation engine analyzes the general liking or purchase behavior of people and helps in predicting their preferences through similarity computations. Similarity can be computed for the user or item based on the algorithm that we implement.

The recommendation engine can be implemented using the collaborative filtering method, content-based method, or a combination of both these methods. In this chapter, we will see the implementation of the **collaborative filtering** method in detail.

The collaborative filtering method can be further classified into user- and item-based methods. The user-based collaborative filtering method is a method where we compute the similarity between the users to arrive at the recommendations, whereas, in the case of an item-based similarity method, we compute the similarity between the items.

Recommendation systems are popular across multiple fields. To be specific, let's consider the e-commerce domain, where, based on the purchase details of various users, we predict the products that could be preferred by users. Amazon, through the implementing recommendation system, increased its sales by about 35%.

In this chapter, we will cover the implementation of the user-based collaborative filtering method, which will include similarity computation using the cosine method and different techniques that will help in improving the recommendation system.

The topics that will be covered in this chapter are as follows:

- Dataset and transformation
- Recommendations using user-based CF
- Recommendations using item-based CF
- Challenges and enhancements

# Dataset and transformation

In this chapter, we will use the dataset that was used in the *Chapter 3, Pattern Discovery*. This dataset has two columns, namely the userID and items. We will consider that the UserID column represents the users and the Items column represents the products purchased by the user.

Let's have a look at the dataset by reading the dataset to the R environment:

```
# reading the dataset
rdata <- read.csv("Data/following.csv")
head(rdata, 10)
```

The output of the preceding code is as follows:

```
> head(data, 10)
   UserID Items
1       1    i1
2       1    i2
3       1    i3
4       1    i4
5       1    i5
6       1    i6
7       1    i7
8       1    i8
9       1    i9
10      1    i10
```

Now, based on the purchase history of all the users, we need to recommend the products that the user might be interested in buying. This can be done by first identifying the similar users and then extracting the new products from the most similar users. We will get into the details of this approach in this chapter.

First of all, in order to build a recommendation system, we need to alter the dataset to a matrix in such a fashion that the items become the row names and the user ID will become the column names. If a user had purchased an item, then the corresponding cell in the matrix will have a value to it; otherwise, it will be zero. It is necessary to convert the dataset into a matrix as it would help us in computing the similarities between the users or items based on the approach we take in order to implement the collaborative filtering algorithm.

We can convert the data into such a matrix format using the following code, where we use the `data.table` package and make use of the `dcast.data.table` function that will help in pivoting the dataset and hence, make it easy for the implementation of the recommendation algorithm:

```
library(data.table)
pivoting <- data.table(rdata)
pivotdata<-dcast.data.table(pivoting, Items ~ UserID, fun.
aggregate=length, value.var="UserID")
head(pivotdata)
```

The output of the preceding code is as follows:

```
> head(pivotdata)
   Items 1 2 3 4 5 6 7 8 9 10 11 12 13 14 15 16 17 18 19 20 21 22 23 24 25 26 27 28 29
1:    11 1 0 0 1 0 0 1 0 0  1  1  0  0  0  1  0  0  0  1  0  0  1  0  1  1  0  0  1  1  0  0
2:   110 1 0 0 1 0 0 1 0 0  1  1  0  0  0  1  0  0  0  1  0  0  1  0  0  1  0  0  1  1  0  0
3:  1100 1 0 0 1 0 0 1 0 0  1  1  0  1  0  0  1  0  0  1  0  0  1  0  0  1  0  0  1  1  0  1
4:  1101 1 0 0 1 0 0 1 0 0  1  1  0  1  1  0  1  0  0  1  0  0  1  0  1  1  0  0  1  1  0  1
5:  1102 1 0 0 1 0 0 1 0 0  1  1  0  1  0  0  1  0  0  1  0  0  1  0  0  1  0  0  1  1  0  1
6:  1103 1 0 0 1 0 0 1 0 0  1  1  0  1  0  0  1  0  0  1  0  0  1  0  0  1  0  0  1  1  0  1
   30 31 32 33 34 35 36 37 38 39 40 41 42 43 44 45 46 47 48 49 50 51 52 53 54 55 56 57
1:  1  0  1  0  0  1  0  1  1  0  0  1  0  1  0  0  0  0  1  1  1  1  1  1  1  0  0  1
2:  1  0  1  0  0  1  0  1  1  0  0  1  0  1  0  1  0  0  1  0  1  0  0  1  1  0  1  1
3:  1  1  1  0  0  1  1  1  1  0  0  1  0  1  0  1  0  0  0  1  1  1  0  1  1  1  0  1
4:  1  1  1  0  0  1  0  1  1  0  1  1  0  1  1  1  0  0  0  1  1  1  0  1  1  1  1  1
5:  1  0  1  0  0  1  0  1  1  0  0  1  0  1  0  1  0  0  0  1  1  0  0  1  1  0  0  1
6:  1  0  1  0  0  1  0  1  1  0  0  1  0  1  0  1  0  0  0  1  1  0  0  1  1  0  0  1
   58 59 60 61 62 63 64 65 66 67 68 69 70 71 72 73 74 75 76 77 78
1:  1  0  0  0  0  0  0  0  1  1  0  0  1  0  0  0  0  0  0  0  0
2:  1  0  0  0  0  0  0  0  1  1  1  0  1  0  0  0  0  0  0  0  1
3:  1  0  1  0  0  0  0  0  1  1  0  1  0  1  0  0  0  0  0  0  0
4:  1  0  1  0  0  0  0  0  1  1  0  1  0  1  0  0  0  0  0  1  1
5:  1  0  1  0  0  0  0  0  1  1  0  1  0  1  0  0  0  0  0  0  0
6:  1  0  1  0  0  0  0  0  1  1  0  1  0  1  0  0  0  0  0  0  0
```

We can see that all the 78 users present in our dataset have become the column names and the items that they purchased have become the row names. The presence of the 1 value means that the user had purchased the corresponding item.

We will save the pivoted file locally as and when the data is large as this process of converting into a matrix is time-consuming. By saving it locally, we can save a lot of time. This conversion activity can be done on a weekly or monthly basis based on the requirement. We will use the following code to save the file in a local system:

```
write.csv(pivotdata, "Data/pivot-follows.csv")
```

Open the saved file and delete the first two columns that represent the rowID and row names. Read this data to be consumed by our recommendation system:

```
ubs<-read.csv("Data/pivot-follows.csv")
```

Thus, after completing the steps involved in the conversion of the dataset into a matrix format, we will now proceed further to the implementation of the user-based collaborative filtering technique.

> After saving the file `pivot-follows`, remember to delete the first two columns that represent the row ID and row names as they are unnecessary while computing the similarity between the users. Alternatively, you can also keep the data untouched in a different data frame so that it can be used for a deeper analysis such as to know which items increased the similarity score between the users.

# Recommendations using user-based CF

In the user-based CF method, we get the recommendations based on the computation of the similarity between the users. There are different methods to compute the similarity between the users. We will see the implementation of similarity computation using the `cosine` method.

The following function computes the cosine similarity between the users. The logic to compute the cosine similarity is mentioned here, but in order to know more about the cosine similarity methodology, refer to the online articles pertaining to cosine similarity. We need to pass the user IDs to be compared to the function. First, we convert the data into a data frame format and omit the products that were not purchased by both the users as including them would bias the similarity score. Then, we compute the cosine similarity for the users. If the pair of users has not bought at least three common products, then we will not be computing the similarity but instead, will make it as zero:

```
# Function to calculate the cosine between two vectors
getCosine <- function(x,y)
{
  dat <- cbind(x,y)
  f <- as.data.frame(dat)
  # Remove the rows with zeros
  datn<- f[-which(rowSums(f==0)>0),]
  if(nrow(datn) > 2)
  {
    this.cosine <- sum(x*y) / (sqrt(sum(x*x)) * sqrt(sum(y*y)))
  }
  else
```

```
{
   this.cosine <- 0
}
   return(this.cosine)
}
```

Now, we will see how to compute the similarity score for all the pairs of users. First, let's create a place holder to hold the similarity scores. The following code will create an empty matrix with the required dimensions:

```
ubs.score  <- matrix(NA, nrow=ncol(ubs),ncol=ncol(ubs),dimnames=list(coln
ames(ubs),colnames(ubs)))
```

With the help of the following code, we will compute the similarity between all the pairs of users in the list. Through the loop, we generate the pair of users and then call the cosine similarity computation function. We will print the counter to get to know the progress while executing the code as follows:

```
# Method: Cosine Similarity
# Lets fill in those empty spaces with cosine similarities
# Loop through the columns
for(i in 1:ncol(ubs)) {
   # Loop through the columns for each column
   for(j in 1:ncol(ubs)) {
      # Fill in placeholder with cosine similarities
      ubs.score[i,j] <- getCosine(data.matrix(ubs[i]),data.matrix(ubs[j]))
   }
   print(i)
}
```

On completing the execution of the preceding dual `for` loop, we get the similarity score for all the user pair combinations in the `ubs.score` matrix. Then, we convert the matrix into a data frame format. We will have a look at the data using the `head` function:

```
ubs.score <- as.data.frame(ubs.score)
head(ubs.score)
```

The output of the preceding code is as follows:

```
> head(ubs.score)
              user1      user10      user11     user12     user13     user14     user15     user16
user1  1.0000000 0.19580898 0.28236052 0.1349454 0.1769335 0.6233715 0.2280273 0.1456352
user10 0.1958090 1.00000000 0.08011224 0.0000000 0.0000000 0.1701144 0.0000000 0.0000000
user11 0.2823605 0.08011224 1.00000000 0.1570059 0.1156661 0.7495534 0.5065378 0.1368579
user12 0.1349454 0.00000000 0.15700586 1.0000000 0.1105580 0.1937676 0.4831677 0.2834303
user13 0.1769335 0.00000000 0.11566606 0.1105580 1.0000000 0.1871323 0.2171560 0.4176056
user14 0.6233715 0.17011439 0.74955344 0.1937676 0.1871323 1.0000000 0.3674254 0.1968160
              user17      user18      user19     user2      user20     user21     user22
user1  0.7009633 0.0000000 0.02171285 0.00000000 0.6973531 0.09473225 0.22115582
user10 0.1568627 0.0000000 0.00000000 0.00000000 0.1560549 0.00000000 0.06757374
user11 0.5195514 0.2248144 0.52468051 0.36547778 0.5661018 0.46348400 0.41413147
user12 0.2069196 0.0000000 0.48107764 0.09913632 0.1940908 0.19854661 0.57047896
user13 0.4313875 0.0000000 0.32612963 0.06028172 0.3808846 0.23283650 0.30972372
user14 0.7638470 0.2121699 0.33378149 0.34492182 0.7964153 0.43208143 0.34485796
              user23      user24      user25     user26     user27     user28     user29     user3
user1  0.7091610 0.2553256 0.02714738 0.5329165 0.5329165 0.30803425 0.3215390 0.0000000
user10 0.1656986 0.0000000 0.00000000 0.1341641 0.1341641 0.00000000 0.1796053 0.0000000
user11 0.3733449 0.2539020 0.49888634 0.7443118 0.7443118 0.00000000 0.9280636 0.3122065
user12 0.2310650 0.1189177 0.09753841 0.4449719 0.4449719 0.00000000 0.1444081 0.0000000
user13 0.5240400 0.1084652 0.09885014 0.4878524 0.4878524 0.08412202 0.1262270 0.0000000
user14 0.6236532 0.2683761 0.47694158 0.7886698 0.7886698 0.23416151 0.7638362 0.2946468
              user30      user31      user32     user33     user34     user35     user36
user1  0.6256946 0.2086817 0.5479155 0.05226414 0.07929518 0.5366866 0.16351928
user10 0.1338258 0.0000000 0.1379401 0.00000000 0.00000000 0.1351132 0.07216878
user11 0.2791312 0.6182611 0.6906683 0.71566466 0.28387105 0.7306349 0.29052553
user12 0.4899644 0.1206538 0.4482534 0.12518734 0.07597372 0.4435933 0.56575238
user13 0.5730813 0.1257700 0.5015831 0.06422839 0.08661987 0.4871751 0.39694209
user14 0.5040977 0.6077995 0.7404702 0.56505120 0.11787819 0.7891414 0.29464677
              user37      user38      user39     user4      user40     user41     user42
user1  0.6997537 0.4739268 0.36364526 0.5329165 0.21005318 0.5329165 0.07629311
user10 0.1565921 0.1265544 0.00000000 0.1341641 0.05688801 0.1341641 0.00000000
user11 0.4727874 0.6301746 0.34047700 0.7443118 0.81008245 0.7443118 0.13352721
user12 0.3068928 0.4245032 0.15075567 0.4449719 0.36020000 0.4449719 0.12182898
user13 0.4467922 0.4959523 0.04583492 0.4878524 0.20859662 0.4878524 0.67598388
user14 0.6959325 0.6862281 0.31187639 0.7886698 0.66451959 0.7886698 0.17184149
```

The preceding output is just a snapshot of the original output.

We will take a look at the other possible methods to compute the similarity score. The other most common method of computing the similarity score is the correlation method. The following function is very similar to the cosine similarity function, but here we use the correlation function to compute the similarity. We compute correlation only for the user pairs who have bought at least three products; otherwise, we make the similarity as zero. By implementing this method, we can slightly improve the accuracy:

```
# Function to calculate the correlation between two vectors
getCor <- function(x)
{
  dat <- x
 f <- as.data.frame(dat)
  datn<- f[-which(rowSums(f==0)>0),]
```

```
if(nrow(datn) > 2)
{
   this.cor <- cor(datn$x,datn$y, method="pearson")
}
else
{
   this.cor <- 0
}
   return(this.cor)
}
```

After computing the similarity score, we need to identify the most similar users. As we did for the similarity score computation, we will first create an empty matrix, which will be the placeholder for the top similar users. The following code will loop through each of the users and filter the similar pairs that have a score greater than the threshold; here, we have set the threshold as 0.1. Then, we use the order function to extract the top similar users. For those users that didn't have a pair with a similarity score above the threshold, there won't be any recommendations.

```
# Get the top 10 neighbours for each
user.neighbours <- matrix(NA, nrow=ncol(ubs.score),ncol=11,dimnames=list(
colnames(ubs.score)))
for(i in 1:ncol(ubs))
{
   # Setting threshold for avoiding zeros
   n <- length(ubs.score[,i])
   thres <- sort(ubs.score[,i],partial=n-10)[n-10]
   if(thres > 0.10)
   {
      # Choosing the top 10 recommendation
      user.neighbours[i,] <- (t(head(n=11,rownames(ubs.
score[order(ubs.score[,i],decreasing=TRUE),][i])))))
   }
   else
   {
user.neighbours[i,] <- ""
   }
}
```

Let's take a look at the top similar users' list. In the following output, ignore the first user that is the same as the original user; it appears because of the self-correlation. The other users are the most similar users sorted based on the similarity score in descending order. Thus, the element that appears first is the most similar user.

```
head(user.neighbours)
```

The output is as follows:

```
> head(user.neighbours, 10)
          [,1]      [,2]      [,3]      [,4]      [,5]      [,6]      [,7]      [,8]
user1   "user1"   "user23"  "user17"  "user37"  "user20"  "user60"  "user8"   "user30"
user10  "user10"  "user71"  "user60"  "user45"  "user1"   "user69"  "user29"  "user8"
user11  "user11"  "user29"  "user40"  "user69"  "user14"  "user26"  "user27"  "user4"
user12  "user12"  "user78"  "user22"  "user5"   "user36"  "user30"  "user47"  "user15"
user13  "user13"  "user42"  "user30"  "user70"  "user66"  "user23"  "user32"  "user38"
user14  "user14"  "user8"   "user69"  "user49"  "user20"  "user35"  "user26"  "user27"
user15  "user15"  "user70"  "user19"  "user32"  "user26"  "user27"  "user4"   "user41"
user16  "user16"  "user5"   "user42"  "user36"  "user30"  "user55"  "user19"  "user47"
user17  "user17"  "user20"  "user37"  "user8"   "user23"  "user49"  "user35"  "user14"
user18  "user18"  "user63"  "user76"  "user46"  "user33"  "user52"  "user49"  "user69"
          [,9]      [,10]     [,11]
user1   "user66"  "user14"  "user49"
user10  "user14"  "user49"  "user23"
user11  "user41"  "user43"  "user50"
user12  "user19"  "user66"  "user70"
user13  "user26"  "user27"  "user4"
user14  "user4"   "user41"  "user43"
user15  "user43"  "user50"  "user53"
user16  "user66"  "user32"  "user22"
user17  "user26"  "user27"  "user4"
user18  "user11"  "user29"  "user20"
```

With the list of the most similar users, now we need to identify a list of the products to recommend to each of the users. In order to get this data, we need to use the preceding output. We will consider the top few similar users and then extract the products bought by these users. Finally, before providing the recommendations, we will check that the recommendations we are going to make have not already been bought by the user.

We will see the implementation of the aforementioned here. In the following `for` loop, we traverse through the users one by one and consider the top two similar users. Then, we identify the items bought by these similar users. We will print the counter in the loop to track the progress while executing the `for` loop:

```
allrec <- ""
# getting the item to recommend
for(i in 1:nrow(user.neighbours))
{
```

```
# Setting threshold for avoiding zeros
for (j in 2:3)
{
    nItem <- user.neighbours[i,j]
    rname <- as.data.frame(nItem)
    rname <- rownames(rname)
    n <- as.numeric(substring(nItem, 5))
    new <- subset(rdata, UserID == n)
    usr <- rname
    rec <- cbind(usr,data.frame(new$Items))
    allrec <- rbind(allrec,rec)
}
print (i)
}
```

After getting the list to be recommended, we will check for the NA values using the `complete.cases` function and rename the column names to match with the format of the original raw dataset:

```
allrec <- allrec[complete.cases(allrec),]
colnames(allrec) <- c("UserID","Items")
head(allrec, 10)
```

The output of the preceding command is as follows:

```
> head(allrec, 10)
     UserID Items
2    user1  i448
3    user1  i470
4    user1  i449
5    user1  i158
6    user1  i124
7    user1   i76
8    user1  i364
9    user1  i337
10   user1  i381
11   user1  i460
```

By comparing this generated list with that of the original raw data, you will understand that our recommendation list includes items that have already been bought by the user. Hence, we need to remove these before making the final recommendations. Use the following code to remove the items that were already bought. As we are implementing this using a SQL query, we need to install the `sqldf` package:

```
install.packages("sqldf")
require(sqldf)
newItems <- sqldf('SELECT * FROM allrec EXCEPT SELECT * FROM rdata')
head(newItems, 10)
```

The output of the preceding command is as follows:

```
> head(newItems, 10)
   UserID Items
1   user1  i143
2   user1  i144
3   user1  i145
4   user1  i146
5   user1  i147
6   user1  i148
7   user1  i149
8   user1  i150
9   user1  i151
10  user1  i152
```

Thus, we are left with the final recommendations for the users. We can even rank the list of recommendations based on the similarity score of the user and popularity of the product itself and can also bring in the concept of segmentation to make it more customized. Many other factors such as marketing, profit margin, and targets can be considered while making the recommendations.

# Recommendations using item-based CF

We have completed the recommendations based on user similarity, and now you will learn how to implement the recommendations based on the item-based filtering methodology. We can implement the item-based CF method with some simple changes to the user-based filtering method.

In the item-based CF method, we identify the similarity between the items. Hence, while pivoting the dataset, we will pivot in such a way that the items become the column names and users become the row names so that we can compute the item similarity and also use the majority of the previous code with simple modifications. The following code can be used to pivot the dataset by making the items as the columns names:

```
library(data.table)
pivoting <- data.table(rdata)
pivotdataItem<-dcast.data.table(pivoting, UserID ~ Items, fun.
aggregate=length, value.var="Items")
colnames(pivotdataItem)
write.csv(pivotdataItem, "Data/pivot-followsItem.csv")
head(pivotdataItem)
```

The output of the preceding command is as follows:

```
> head(pivotdataItem)
   UserID i1 i10 i100 i101 i102 i103 i104 i105 i106 i107 i108 i109 i11 i110 i111
1:  user1  1   1    1    1    1    1    1    1    1    1    1    1   1    1    1
2: user10  0   0    0    0    0    0    0    0    0    0    0    0   0    0    0
3: user11  0   0    1    1    1    1    1    1    1    1    1    0   1    1    1
4: user12  0   0    0    1    0    0    0    1    0    0    0    0   0    0    0
5: user13  1   1    0    0    0    0    0    0    0    0    0    1   0    0    0
6: user14  0   0    1    1    1    1    1    1    1    1    1    0   1    1    1
   i112 i113 i114 i115 i116 i117 i118 i119 i12 i120 i121 i122 i123 i124 i125 i126
1:    1    1    1    1    1    1    1    1   1    1    1    1    1    1    1    1
2:    0    0    0    0    0    0    0    0   0    0    0    0    0    0    0    0
3:    1    1    1    1    1    1    1    1   0    1    1    1    1    1    1    1
4:    0    0    0    0    0    0    1    1   0    0    0    0    1    0    0    0
5:    0    0    0    0    0    0    0    0   1    0    0    0    0    0    0    0
6:    1    1    1    1    1    1    1    1   0    1    1    1    1    1    1    1
   i127 i128 i129 i13 i130 i131 i132 i133 i134 i135 i136 i137 i138 i139 i14 i140
1:    1    1    1   1    1    1    1    1    1    1    1    1    1    1   1    1
2:    0    0    0   0    0    0    0    0    0    0    0    0    0    0   0    0
3:    1    1    1   0    1    1    1    1    1    1    1    1    1    1   0    1
4:    1    0    0   0    0    0    0    0    0    0    0    0    0    0   0    0
5:    0    0    0   0    0    0    0    0    1    0    0    0    0    0   0    0
6:    1    1    1   1    1    1    1    1    1    1    1    1    1    1   1    1
   i141 i142 i143 i144 i145 i146 i147 i148 i149 i15 i150 i151 i152 i153 i154 i155
1:    1    1    0    0    0    0    0    0    0   1    0    0    0    0    0    0
2:    0    0    0    0    1    0    0    0    0   0    0    0    0    0    0    0
3:    1    1    1    1    1    1    1    1    1   0    1    1    1    1    1    1
4:    0    0    0    1    1    0    1    0    0   0    0    0    0    0    0    0
5:    1    0    0    0    0    0    0    0    0   0    0    0    0    0    0    0
6:    1    1    1    1    1    1    1    1    1   1    1    1    1    1    1    1
```

The preceding output is just a snapshot of the original output.

This can be saved locally as it is a time-consuming process, and, as mentioned in the previous section, we need to remove the first two columns and then read the modified data to compute the similarity between the items using the `getCosine` function, which was also explained in the user-based recommendation section.

We can use the following code to identify the similarity between the items:

```
ibs<-read.csv("Data/pivot-followsItem.csv")
head(ibs)
colnames(ibs)
# Create a placeholder dataframe listing item vs. item
ibs.score   <- matrix(NA, nrow=ncol(ibs),ncol=ncol(ibs),dimnames=list(coln
ames(ibs),colnames(ibs)))
# Lets fill in those empty spaces with cosine similarities
# Loop through the columns
for(i in 1:ncol(ibs)) {
  # Loop through the columns for each column
  for(j in 1:ncol(ibs)) {
    # Fill in placeholder with cosine similarities
    ibs.score[i,j] <- getCosine(data.matrix(ibs[i]),data.matrix(ibs[j]))
  }
  print(i)
}
ibs.score <- as.data.frame(ibs.score)
```

After computing the similarity scores, we can now filter out the top similar items using the following code, which was also explained in detail under the user-based recommendation system:

```
item.neighbours <- matrix(NA, nrow=ncol(ibs.score),ncol=11,dimnames=list(
colnames(ibs.score)))
for(i in 1:ncol(ubs))
{
  # Setting threshold for avoiding zeros
  n <- length(ibs.score[,i])
  thres <- sort(ibs.score[,i],partial=n-10)[n-10]
  if(thres > 0.10)
  {
    # Choosing the top 10 recommendation
```

```
    item.neighbours[i,] <- (t(head(n=11,rownames(ibs.score[order(ibs.
score[,i],decreasing=TRUE),][i])))))
  }
  else
  {
    item.neighbours[i,] <- ""
  }
}
head(item.neighbours, 10)
```

The output of the following command is as follows:

```
> head(item.neighbours, 10)
       [,1]    [,2]   [,3]    [,4]   [,5]    [,6]     [,7]    [,8]    [,9]    [,10]    [,11]
i1     "i1"    "i2"   "i23"   "i3"   "i12"   "i499"   "i5"    "i7"    "i24"   "i500"   "i18"
i10    "i10"   "i11"  "i12"   "i29"  "i14"   "i16"    "i4"    "i13"   "i499"  "i19"    "i7"
i100   "i100"  "i99"  "i104"  "i102" "i103"  "i96"    "i98"   "i97"   "i85"   "i111"   "i115"
i101   "i101"  "i104" "i100"  "i99"  "i90"   "i111"   "i106"  "i57"   "i84"   "i102"   "i103"
i102   "i102"  "i103" "i96"   "i98"  "i99"   "i87"    "i89"   "i104"  "i97"   "i85"    "i100"
i103   "i102"  "i103" "i96"   "i98"  "i99"   "i87"    "i89"   "i104"  "i97"   "i85"    "i100"
i104   "i104"  "i100" "i99"   "i102" "i103"  "i96"    "i98"   "i97"   "i115"  "i87"    "i89"
i105   "i105"  "i106" "i116"  "i115" "i108"  "i57"    "i95"   "i107"  "i113"  "i117"   "i118"
i106   "i106"  "i116" "i109"  "i112" "i108"  "i114"   "i102"  "i103"  "i96"   "i98"    "i107"
i107   "i107"  "i113" "i116"  "i97"  "i117"  "i111"   "i115"  "i106"  "i108"  "i114"   "i99"
```

Thus, we get the recommendations based on the item-based similarity methodology.

# Challenges and enhancements

Having seen the implementation of the recommendation system based on the item-based and user-based similarity methodologies, we will explore some of the challenges:

- Recommendation systems in general have the cold-start problem, that is, the algorithm would work fine when there is enough data, but with a lack of data, the accuracy would go for a toss

- People's behavior might change with time or there could be behavior that is seasonal, and hence, these might have an impact on the recommendations

General methods to improve the accuracy are as follows:

- While computing the similarity between the pairs (user or item), consider only the rows where at least one of the items of the pair has an entry. By this method, we will remove all the (0,0) pairs and hence could arrive at a more accurate similarity score.

- Compute the similarities using multiple methods and identify the method that best suits the data.

- Go for the hybrid approach where you combine multiple methods such as user-based, item-based, and content-based approaches, and then combine them to arrive at the final recommendations, which generally would have a better accuracy.

- While implementing the recommendation system, segment the data into different groups and compute the similarity instead of considering all the data to arrive at the recommendations.

- Rank the final recommendations based on the metrics that are important to the business; in case of e-commerce, rank them based on the popularity, profit margin, and so on.

# Summary

In this chapter, we covered the concepts of the recommendation system using the user-based and item-based methodologies. In the process, you learned techniques to convert the data into a format ready to be consumed by the recommendation algorithm and to compute the similarity score using both the cosine similarity and the correlation methods. Additionally, the methodology to compute is explained, empowering the reader to try similar methodology and finally, arrive at the final recommendation list. In the end, we touched on the various techniques that can be used to improve the accuracy of our recommendation engine.

The recommendation engine is a popular technique used across multiple industries and has also proved in bringing monetary benefit to the business. For example, the e-commerce industry uses this to provide recommendations to the users on the products that they might be interested in buying based on their behavior as well as other similar users' behavior, thereby increasing the revenue.

In the next chapter, we will cover visualization techniques to create interactive dashboards for better communication of insights to a business user.

# 8
# Communicating Data Analysis

The most important step of the data analysis process is the communication of the analysis to the user. It is very essential to customize the reports based on the role and need of the users. All your analysis is worthless if it is not communicated in the right way.

Visualization is a representation of the data in the graphical or pictorial format, which generally attracts the attention of the people. R is a powerful tool not only for the analysis and implementation of machine learning algorithms, but also for the visualization and communication of the analysis through the creation of interactive dashboards.

The data visualization has been adopted by people and organizations across the world as a means to communicate. The most common example is that we understand the performance of a vehicle through its dashboard.

We will cover interesting visualization using the `googleVis` package and also the creation of an interactive dashboard using R Shiny.

The topics that will be covered in this chapter are as follows:

- Dataset
- Plotting using the googleVis package
- Creating an interactive dashboard using Shiny

# Dataset

In this chapter, we will use the dataset that was used in *Chapter 4, Segmentation Using Clustering*. This dataset captures various data about the various countries around the world. We will use a few of these column vectors to learn about data visualization and communication. As we have already seen the structure of the dataset, we will move on to the concepts.

# Plotting using the googleVis package

We will take a look at one interesting visualization using the googleVis package. First, we need to install the package and load it to the R environment using the following code:

```
install.packages("googleVis")

library(googleVis)
```

We will now read a dataset that can be visualized using the googleVis package. From the worlddata dataset, we will consider the country and co2_emissions columns. The following code will read the dataset with all the columns and then select the required columns by specifying their names. We will then remove the rows with the NA values:

```
data <- read.csv("Data/worlddata.csv")

newdata <- data[,c("country","co2_emissions")]

newdata <- na.omit(newdata)

head(newdata, 10)
```

The output of the preceding command is as follows:

```
> head(newdata, 10)
                 country co2_emissions
1                  Aruba          2439
2                Andorra           491
3            Afghanistan         12251
4                 Angola         29710
5                Albania          4668
6              Arab world       1704418
7    United Arab Emirates        178484
8              Argentina        190035
9                Armenia          4961
11  Antigua and Barbuda           513
```

We have now got the carbon dioxide emissions for all the countries. Let's try to plot this on the world map itself using the gvisGeoChart function. We need to pass the dataset that has to be plotted, the locationvar parameter should be set to the column that holds the country name, the colorvar parameter should be specified with the column based on which the color coding needs to be implemented, and finally, we need to pass the map projection on which the data needs to be plotted to the options parameter. Moreover, the width and height parameters specify the size of the plot:

```
GeoPlot<- gvisGeoChart(newdata, locationvar="country",
  colorvar="co2_emissions",
  options=list(projection="kavrayskiy-vii", width=1000, height=700))
plot(GeoPlot)
```

The plot function will open the following output in the default browser:

On hovering the mouse, we will get the actual emission values for the countries. Thus, this is an interesting plot using the googleVis package.

Let's explore a few more visualizations using the googleVis package. We will consider only the top 5% of the data based on the `co2_emissions` column. We will be implementing a bar chart using the `gvisBarChart` function, column chart using the `gvisColumnChart` function, area chart using the `gvisAreaChart` function, and pie chart using the `gvisPieChart` function, as follows:

```
Filtereddata <- newdata[newdata$co2_emissions > quantile(newdata$co2_
emissions,prob=1-5/100),]
head(Filtereddata)
# bar Chart
Bar <- gvisBarChart(Filtereddata)
plot(Bar)
```

The output of the preceding command is as follows:

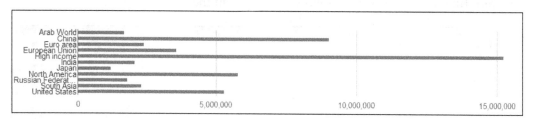

Let's check the representation of the data using a column chart:

```
# Column Chart
Clmn <- gvisColumnChart(Filtereddata)
plot(Clmn)
```

The output of the preceding command is as follows:

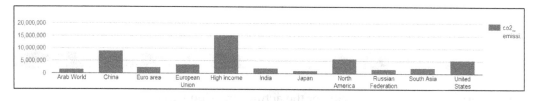

Let's check the representation of the data using a area chart:

```
Area <- gvisAreaChart(Filtereddata)
plot(Area)
```

The output of the preceding command is as follows:

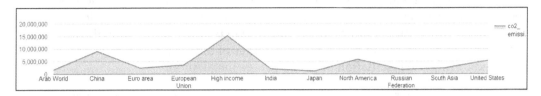

Let's check the representation of the data using a pie chart:

```
Pie <- gvisPieChart(Filtereddata)
plot(Pie)
```

The output of the preceding command is as follows:

In order to learn about a few more interesting visualizations using the googleVis package, refer to the following URL:

```
https://cran.r-project.org/web/packages/googleVis/vignettes/
googleVis_examples.html
```

It holds a working example of various plotting methods. We will now move on to the creation of an interactive dashboard using Shiny.

# Creating an interactive dashboard using Shiny

**Shiny** is a web application framework for R. We can create an interactive dashboard using Shiny. We will see the implementation of a sample dashboard using R and Shiny in detail.

In order to create interactive dashboards using Shiny from R, we need to install and load the shiny package in R:

```
install.packages("shiny")
library(shiny)
```

After installing and loading the `shiny` package in R, you can check the `\win-library\3.2\shiny\examples` path in the R folder where the folders and files related to the packages are saved. The R folder would mostly be present in the program files; if R doesn't have the administrative privilege to write to the program files, it would be present in the `Documents` folder or any other custom folder specified during the installation or first-package installation.

In the `examples` folder, you can see various sample apps that have been developed. We can create a new folder and start the development of a new application. Alternatively, you can also run the example code using the `runExample` function. In order to run the `01_hello` app, we need to use the `runExample("01_hello")` command.

The Shiny app development has two important components, namely, the server script and UI script. Let's create a new folder named `App` and use it for the interactive dashboard app development. Remember that the folder name will be used to execute the app.

The UI script holds the layout and appearance information of the app and it should be named `ui.R`. Copy and paste the following code in the `ui.R` file:

```
shinyUI(navbarPage("Interactive Dashboard",
  tabPanel("Scatter Plot",
    plotOutput("plot")
  ),
  tabPanel("Summary Report",
    verbatimTextOutput("summary")
  ),
  tabPanel("Data",
    dataTableOutput("table")
  )
))
```

The preceding UI code creates three different tabs for the dashboard namely `Scatter Plot`, `Summary Report`, and `Data`. From the preceding UI code, we can understand that the first tab contains a plot, the second one contains a test output, and the third tab contains a tabular output.

The server script holds the information to build the app. Let's see in detail how we can populate the three tabs using the server-side script. We need to name this file `server.R`. Copy and paste the following code in the `server.R` file:

```
shinyServer(function(input, output, session) {
  # First Tab
  output$plot <- renderPlot({
    data <- read.csv("Data/worlddata.csv")
```

```
    data <- data[,c("gdp_in_millions","co2_emissions")]
    data <- na.omit(data)
    data <- data[data$gdp_in_millions >
      quantile(data$gdp_in_millions,prob=1-10/100),]
    plot(data, type="p")
  })

  # Second Tab
  output$summary <- renderPrint({
    data <- read.csv("Data/worlddata.csv")
    data <- data[,c("gdp_in_millions","co2_emissions")]
    data <- na.omit(data)
    data <- data[data$gdp_in_millions >
      quantile(data$gdp_in_millions,prob=1-10/100),]
    summary(data)
  })
  # Third Tab
  output$table <- renderDataTable({
    data <- read.csv("Data/worlddata.csv")
    data <-
      data[,c("country","gdp_in_millions","co2_emissions")]
    data <- na.omit(data)
    data <- data[data$gdp_in_millions >
      quantile(data$gdp_in_millions,prob=1-10/100),]
    data
  }, options=list(pageLength=10))
})
```

The `renderPlot` function in the server script will implement the scatter plot. From the `worlddata` dataset, we read `gdp_in_millions` and `co2_emissions` columns, and then we remove the NA rows and consider only the top 10% based on the `gdp_in_millions` column for better visualization. Finally, we use the `plot` function with the `type` parameter set to pin order to make the scatter plot.

We use the `renderPrint` function to populate the second tab. This function is exactly the same in terms of the formatting but we use the `summary` function to get a summary detail about the dataset. The last `renderDataTable` function will print the entire dataset in the third tab. The only difference here is that we hold an additional column i.e. `country` for the easier interpretation of the results.

Thus, we explored the server and `ui` script for our dashboard. Now, in order to activate the dashboard, we need to execute the following code. Remember that the name of our folder is `App`, hence we will use it as a parameter in the `runExample` function. It will open the dashboard in the browser.

```
runExample("App")
```

> Remember that the `ui` and `server` scripts need to be placed under the folder named `App` in the examples folder according to the preceding command. Additionally, remember to set the directory location according to the location of the dataset; in the preceding example, the directory will have a folder named `Data` that will hold the actual dataset.

Let's have a look at the dashboard that we just created.

TAB 1 is given as follows:

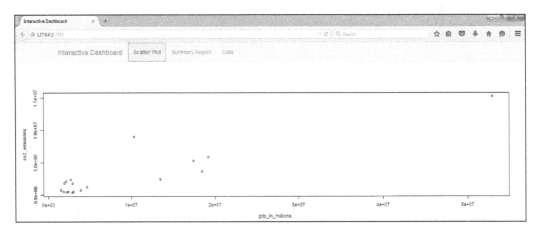

TAB 2 is given as follows:

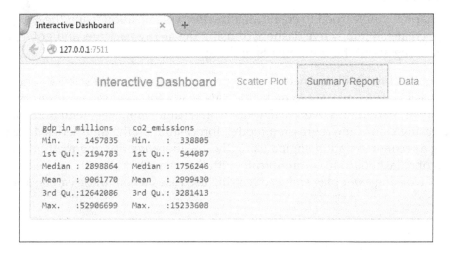

TAB 3 is given as follows:

Thus, we created a simple interactive dashboard using R and Shiny. In order to know about the creation of interactive dashboards in detail, refer to `http://shiny.rstudio.com/tutorial/`.

In the preceding URL, you will find a few working examples along with the code and output in addition to the tutorials.

# Summary

In this chapter, you learned to create an attractive visualization using the `googleVis` package, create an interactive dashboard using the `shiny` package, and got a good understanding about the components of the app.

Finally, in this book, you learned some of the most essential data science concepts, such as basic data formatting to make the data ready for analysis, exploratory data analysis, pattern discovery using the Apriori algorithm, segmentation using the clustering algorithm, regression model, forecasting on the time series dataset, building a recommendation engine using the collaborative filtering method, and the creation of a dashboard to communicate with the user. Overall, you learned all of this with working examples and also real-life use cases where these can be applied.

# Index

## A

**aggregation operations**
  about 13
  maximum 14
  mean 13
  median 13
  minimum 14
  standard deviation 14
  sum 13
**Apriori analysis 47, 48**
**Apriori sequence analysis**
  about 55, 56
  business cases 58
  reference link 56
**arithmetic operations 11**
**association rule analysis, parameters**
  confidence 48, 49
  lift 48, 49
  support 48
**autoregressive integrated moving average (ARIMA)**
  about 91
  order parameter 99
  used, for forecasting 99-101

## B

**bivariate analysis 33-35**
**box plot**
  plotting, for descriptive statistics 26
**break control structure 16**

**built-in dataset**
  using 42-45

## C

**Cassandra 5**
**centroid-based clustering 64-66**
**clustering**
  about 59
  business use cases 73
  datasets, formatting 61-63
  datasets, reading 61-63
  datasets, using 60
**clusters**
  ideal number, obtaining 64-66
  implementing, K-means
    algorithm used 66, 67
  visualizing 68, 69
**collaborative filtering method 107**
**comma-separated values (CSV) format 2**
**connectivity-based clustering**
  about 69, 70
  visualizing 71, 72
**control structures**
  about 14
  break 15
  for 15
  if and else 15
  next 16
  repeat 15
  return 16
  while 15
**cross-tabulation analysis 36, 37**

# D

**data**
  preparing, for analysis  17, 18
  reading, from database  3-6
  reading, from different source  2, 3
**dataframe  9**
**data operations**
  aggregation operations  13
  arithmetic operations  11
  performing  10
  string operations  12
**data preprocessing**
  techniques  9, 10
**dataset**
  plotting  51
**data types**
  about  6
  dataframe  9
  factors  8
  list  8
  matrix  7
  variable data types  6-8
  vector  7
**data visualization**
  about  121
  dataset, using  122
  interactive dashboard, creating
    with Shiny  125-129
  plotting, googleVis package used  122-125
**DBI driver  4**
**descriptive statistics**
  about  23-26
  box plot  26

# E

**ensemble models**
  building  87
  highly correlated values, removing  89
  NA values, replacing with mean or
    median  87, 88
  outliers, removing  89, 90
**exploratory data analysis  21**

# F

**factors  8**
**forecasting**
  about  91
  accuracy, improving  105
  autoregressive integrated moving average
    (ARIMA), using  99-101
  datasets, using  92-95
  Holt-Winters, using  101-105
  patterns, extracting  95-98
**for loop  15**

# G

**googleVis package**
  reference link  125
  used, for plotting data
    visualization  122-125
**graphical analysis  38, 39**

# H

**Hadoop  5**
**hierarchical clustering.** *See*
    **connectivity-based clustering**
**Holt-Winters**
  about  91
  URL  105
  used, for forecasting  101-105

# I

**if and else control structure  15**
**inferential statistics  28-30**
**interactive dashboard**
  creating, Shiny used  125-129
**item-based CF method**
  used, for implementing recommendation
    system  116-119

# J

**JDBC driver**
  URL  4

## K

**K-means algorithm**
about 64
used, for cluster implementation 66, 67

## L

**linear regression**
about 83-86
evaluating 86
**list** 8
**logistic regression**
about 79, 80
evaluating 81-83

## M

**matrix** 7
**MongoDB** 5
**multivariate analysis**
about 36
cross-tabulation analysis 36, 37
graphical analysis 38, 39

## N

**next control structure** 16

## O

**Oracle** 4

## P

**pattern discovery** 41
**PostgreSQL** 4
**public dataset**
references 27

## R

**Random Forest** 87
**recommendation engine** 107
**recommendation system**
challenges 119, 120
dataset, using 108-110

enhancements 119, 120
implementing, item-based CF
method used 116-119
implementing, user-based CF
method used 110-116
**regression analysis 75**
**regression models**
accuracy, improving 87
dataset, sampling 78, 79
datasets, using 76, 77
ensemble models, building 87
linear regression 83-86
logistic regression 79, 80
Random Forest 87
Support Vector Machine (SVM) 87
**repeat control structure 16**
**return control structure 16**
**rules**
filtering 49, 50
plotting 52, 53
references 57
results, checking 56, 57

## S

**SAS 5**
**Seasonal Decomposition of Time 95**
**sensitivity and specificity**
reference link 83
**sequential dataset 53-55**
**Shiny**
about 125
reference link 129
used, for creating interactive
dashboard 125-129
**SPSS 5**
**SQL Server 4**
**Stata 5**
**stl function**
about 95
reference link 98
**string operations 12**
**Support Vector Machine (SVM) 87**
**Systat 5**

# T

time series forecasting 91
Titanic dataset
  URL 22
  using 22
  variables 22
transactional datasets
  about 42
  building 45, 46
  built-in dataset, using 42-45

# U

univariate analysis 30-33
unsupervised learning 59
user-based CF method
  used, for implementing recommendation
      system 110-116

# V

variable data types 6, 8
vector 7

# W

while loop 15

## Thank you for buying
# R Data Science Essentials

## About Packt Publishing

Packt, pronounced 'packed', published its first book, *Mastering phpMyAdmin for Effective MySQL Management*, in April 2004, and subsequently continued to specialize in publishing highly focused books on specific technologies and solutions.

Our books and publications share the experiences of your fellow IT professionals in adapting and customizing today's systems, applications, and frameworks. Our solution-based books give you the knowledge and power to customize the software and technologies you're using to get the job done. Packt books are more specific and less general than the IT books you have seen in the past. Our unique business model allows us to bring you more focused information, giving you more of what you need to know, and less of what you don't.

Packt is a modern yet unique publishing company that focuses on producing quality, cutting-edge books for communities of developers, administrators, and newbies alike. For more information, please visit our website at www.packtpub.com.

## About Packt Open Source

In 2010, Packt launched two new brands, Packt Open Source and Packt Enterprise, in order to continue its focus on specialization. This book is part of the Packt Open Source brand, home to books published on software built around open source licenses, and offering information to anybody from advanced developers to budding web designers. The Open Source brand also runs Packt's Open Source Royalty Scheme, by which Packt gives a royalty to each open source project about whose software a book is sold.

## Writing for Packt

We welcome all inquiries from people who are interested in authoring. Book proposals should be sent to author@packtpub.com. If your book idea is still at an early stage and you would like to discuss it first before writing a formal book proposal, then please contact us; one of our commissioning editors will get in touch with you.

We're not just looking for published authors; if you have strong technical skills but no writing experience, our experienced editors can help you develop a writing career, or simply get some additional reward for your expertise.

## R for Data Science

ISBN: 978-1-78439-086-0          Paperback: 364 pages

Learn and explore the fundamentals of data science with R

1. Familiarize yourself with R programming packages and learn how to utilize them effectively.

2. Learn how to detect different types of data mining sequences.

3. A step-by-step guide to understanding R scripts and the ramifications of your changes.

## R Data Analysis Cookbook

ISBN: 978-1-78398-906-5          Paperback: 342 pages

Over 80 recipes to help you breeze through your data analysis projects using R

1. Analyse data with ready-to-use and customizable recipes.

2. Discover convenient functions to speed-up your work and data files.

3. Demystifies several R packages that seasoned data analysts regularly use.

Please check **www.PacktPub.com** for information on our titles

# R Data Visualization Cookbook

ISBN: 978-1-78398-950-8          Paperback: 236 pages

Over 80 recipes to analyze data and create stunning visualizations with R

1. Create animated and interactive plots to help you communicate and explore data.

2. Utilize various R packages to generate graphs, manipulate data, and create beautiful presentations.

3. Learn to interpret data and tell a story using this step-by-step guide to data visualization.

# Building Interactive Graphs with ggplot2 and Shiny [Video]

ISBN: 978-1-78328-433-7          Duration: 01:51 hours

Build stunning graphics and interactive visuals for real-time data analysis and visualization with ggplot2 and Shiny

1. Generate complex interactive web pages using R and produce publication-ready graphics in a principled manner.

2. Use aesthetics effectively to map your data into graphical elements.

3. Customize your graphs according to your specific needs without wasting time on programming issues.

Please check **www.PacktPub.com** for information on our titles

www.ingramcontent.com/pod-product-compliance
Lightning Source LLC
Chambersburg PA
CBHW060146060326
40690CB00018B/3998